S0-AAC-719

TEACHERS THAT SEXUALLY ABUSE STUDENTS

HOW TO ORDER THIS BOOK

BY PHONE: 800-233-9936 or 717-291-5609, 8AM–5PM Eastern Time

BY FAX: 717-295-4538

BY MAIL: Order Department
Technomic Publishing Company, Inc.
851 New Holland Avenue, Box 3535
Lancaster, PA 17604, U.S.A.

BY CREDIT CARD: American Express, VISA, MasterCard

BY WWW SITE: http://www.techpub.com

PERMISSION TO PHOTOCOPY–POLICY STATEMENT

Authorization to photocopy items for internal or personal use, or the internal or personal use of spe-
cific clients, is granted by Technomic Publishing Co., Inc. provided that the base fee of US $3.00 per
copy, plus US $ .25 per page is paid directly to Copyright Clearance Center, 222 Rosewood Drive,
Danvers, MA 01923, USA. For those organizations that have been granted a photocopy license by
CCC, a separate system of payment has been arranged. The fee code for users of the Transactional
Reporting Service is 1-56676/98 $5.00 + $ .25.

TEACHERS THAT SEXUALLY ABUSE STUDENTS

An Administrative & Legal Guide

Stephen Rubin, Ph.D.

Professor of Psychology
Whitman College

John S. Biggs, J.D.

Staff Attorney
Peninsula School District

TECHNOMIC
PUBLISHING CO., INC.

LANCASTER · BASEL

Teachers That Sexually Abuse Students
aTECHNOMIC ẗublication

Technomic Publishing Company, Inc.
851 New Holland Avenue, Box 3535
Lancaster, Pennsylvania 17604 U.S.A.

Copyright ©1999 by Technomic Publishing Company, Inc.
All rights reserved

No part of this publication may be reproduced, stored in a
retrieval system, or transmitted, in any form or by any means,
electronic, mechanical, photocopying, recording, or otherwise,
without the prior written permission of the publisher.

Printed in the United States of America
10   9   8   7   6   5   4   3   2   1

Main entry under title:
    Teachers That Sexually Abuse Students: An Administrative & Legal Guide

A Technomic Publishing Company book
Bibliography: p.
Includes index p. 217

Library of Congress Catalog Card No. 98-85050
ISBN No. 1-56676-627-3

To schoolchildren everywhere:
May your childhood be fun and safe
and may your teachers be wonderful mentors

TEACHERS That Sexually Abuse Students is timely—and long overdue. What separates this book from others on sexual abuse is that it combines thorough examination with a plan of action for educators in schools.

The book's point–counterpoint style provides the reader with insights from contrasting perspectives—that of a lawyer and that of a psychologist. Nonetheless, despite the differing backgrounds of the authors, the text shows why indifference to the sexual abuse of students by school personnel is never an option.

Drawing on many accounts, the book's approach is at once wide and deep. *Teachers That Sexually Abuse Students* probes the causal factors of abuse and also provides guidelines for recognizing and preventing the problem, especially in hiring, training, and retaining staff. Here one finds a guide on how to deal with school personnel, law enforcement agencies, staff training, and harassment.

The authors' consideration of parents creates an understanding of what parents may feel—and why. The helpful points provided for parents serve as excellent ways to recognize the early warning signs of sexual abuse.

This book should be required reading for prospective or practicing teachers and administrators, for those serving in the human resource field, and for parents of school-aged children. Filled with insight and sadness, this work cannot be read passively. It provides real solutions to a subject charged with emotion, denial, and secretiveness.

Gratitude is due the authors, Rubin and Biggs, for addressing a sensitive issue with dispassionate assessment and concrete plans of action.

ROGER L. LEHNERT
Superintendent

THIS text is primarily intended for school administrators who supervise teachers and support staff in public or private schools. If you are one of those persons, you are on the front line in society's effort to protect students from sexual abuse. You are expected to protect our youth from the pedophile—the person who sees children as his or her preferred sexual object. Because the children are there, these persons continue to be drawn to our schools, and you are the keeper of those children. This book is intended to help you achieve society's expectations.

Your authors are somewhat of an odd couple. Dr. Stephen Rubin is a practicing clinical psychologist and professor of psychology at Whitman College, a small, prestigious, liberal arts college in Washington State. He is a former grade school teacher and school psychologist, and is currently a state-licensed sex offender treatment provider who maintains an active caseload of persons who have exhibited symptoms consistent with pedophilia. He is also a long-time critic of the traditional manner in which K–12 educational institutions, both public and private, have responded to the threat posed by the teacher who sexually abuses students (TSAS). This identification includes both pedophiles and non-pedophiles.

John Biggs is a school attorney who began his school-law career defending teachers. He has since been involved in the discharge of many teachers who have abused students. Mr. Biggs has written extensively on school administration and the law. He is currently the general counsel of a public school district in the state of Washington.

On occasion, Dr. Rubin and Mr. Biggs have been on opposite sides of particular issues—Mr. Biggs attempting to dismiss and Dr. Rubin arguing to retain an employee. On other occasions they have found themselves on the same side. But, although they have agreed to disagree, they both believe the topic addressed here is a serious one which deserves your utmost attention.

Sexual abuse is not a state of mind. At least two persons are required and, to a certain extent, both must participate. Therefore, this book not only focuses on the indicia of the pedophile but also those of the victim. In particular, we examine the earlier sexualization of kids, the effect of broken homes, the increasing sexuality in our society, and the impact of tacit societal acceptance of gay and lesbian values.

The authors warrant that the vignettes presented in this text report real life events that have occurred in the K–12 school setting. Generally, these situations personally involved one or both of the authors. In two cases, however, the vignette is based upon news accounts accessed by the authors from news of general circulation. The authors assume all risks associated with the clinical presentation of these events. Consistent with this assumption, the authors have chosen to avoid potential defamation claims and unnecessary injury to business reputation by most often changing names and locations (except in actual court cases) but warrant to both Technomic Publishing Company and readers that no substantive factual patterns have been changed. For reasons stated, readers must attribute to the authors rather than the authors' sources. Technomic Publishing Company accepts the authors' foregoing representations and in electing to publish, has relied upon the authors' assumptions of risk. Technomic Publishing Company disclaims all responsibility for the factual presentations made by the authors.

WHAT THIS BOOK IS ABOUT

John S. Biggs: It is hard to get rid of a teacher—and, it should be! But they are not gods or sacred cows. They are public employees entrusted with the health, safety, and welfare of our children. The overwhelming majority are dedicated, hard-working folks whose values reflect our society and who are ideal role models to our children. But, a few are in our schools with another sort of agenda altogether, and their presence makes life difficult for everyone else. The siren songs continue: We must give them the benefit of the doubt! Surely everyone is innocent until proven guilty! We must give them due process! We must respect differing values and sexual preferences! We must protect the employees "contract" rights! We must make a clear distinction between their rights and responsibilities at work and their private lives and not intrude into their private lives, etc., etc. I believe that, eventually, we must recognize that <u>strict pro-employee</u> implementation of all of these concepts is exposing our youth to increasing risk and that some among us are taking advantage. Eventually, we have to return to the historical concept of administrator discretion to be suspicious and then develop a cadre of administrators who will protect both the children and the employees when necessary—in that order.

Stephen Rubin: Washington State recently enacted a <u>"Violent Predator" Law,</u> which provides that persons convicted of crimes involving sexual abuse could be held indefinitely, not for crimes that they had committed and served their sentences for, but for crimes they were likely to commit in the future. This is a far cry from the concept of innocent until proven guilty. The concept of the nuclear family has deteriorated to the point where less than fifty percent of children will be raised by both of their biological parents. As a result, more adults from outside the family unit will be involved in the children's lives. We must reexamine the role of the teacher and the school system and ask whether teachers are now being asked to relate to children in areas outside their training and perhaps beyond the historical teacher–student relationship. Are we training our staff too little? Are we asking too much?

Is it the role of the school system to help teachers deal with personal attraction to students? I believe so. There is a natural attraction of teachers to students and students to teachers. This has its advantages and disadvantages. The attraction can and does generate the most exciting learning environment, yet has the potential to devastate the lives of everyone involved. School systems must face these situations and neither seek a scapegoat nor adopt the head-in-the-sand mentality of the ostrich. These situations have always been, and will always be, a part of the educational environment.

CHAPTER 1

Historical Perspective

AS we consider the teacher's position in the American community over the past 150 years, we notice some important, unique aspects. The teacher was one of the central role models and pillars of the community, a symbol of both education and reason. A community with a schoolhouse and a teacher was considered civilized. The teacher represented culture. This, however, was disproportionate to the monetary compensation that the community paid to the teacher. The community expected a great deal from a "school marm" or "principal." In 1902 the board of trustees of a small Baptist school adjudged a young woman incompetent, due to her extracurricular activities, which included attending a minstrel show, going to a cafe, and socializing with gentlemen (Winks, 1982). Winks also points out that, in 1932, a teacher who worked in her husband's beer garden was dismissed because she no longer commanded the respect and goodwill of the community.

The teacher had not only to be a "paragon of virtue" but also had to maintain the appearance of virtue. In another case, referenced in the Winks' paper, a messy divorce between a teacher and spouse was used as grounds for dismissal. Winks did point out that these cases were usually from rural communities, which seem to have a more intimate relationship with their teachers. For example, in *Richards v. School Board,* a 1915 Oregon case, a female teacher was dismissed for getting married, and even as late as 1970, in *Ramsey v. Hopkins,* an Alabama case, a teacher was dismissed for wearing a moustache. These historical examples show the application of a *local standard* of morality.

In 1973, the California Supreme Court upheld the dismissal of a teacher who had admitted to oral copulation at a swingers' party. No one suggested that her private sexual behavior directly interfered with her duties as a classroom teacher of the mentally retarded.

Because a state supreme court issued this decision, it became a *statewide standard* of morality, equally applicable in urban and rural areas. Clearly, even as the courts became more involved and sought to provide equal protection, there have continued to be cases where the overall moral character of the teacher was the major issue in teacher dismissal. Therefore, as we proceed, we need to consider both the safety of the students and the teacher's right to a private life.

Into the 1950s, and even today in some rural areas, teaching was viewed as a profession akin to law, medicine, or the ministry. Those who were called to teach were expected to be persons of high moral character, with good values and good taste. Back then, as now, school administrators tended to be persons who had previously taught. Compensation levels, as compared to other professions, tended to be relatively low, society expecting those who served to gain personal satisfaction from the impact they had on the learning and character development of their students. In consideration of the lower income levels and in order to be consistent with the view of teachers and administrators as models of the community's values, we treated these persons as being *in loco parentis* (in place of the parent) to the youth in their charge. Consistent with this theory or approach, children were taught to respect and obey their parents and their teachers. When a dispute arose between a student and teacher or administrator, corporal punishment was often given and disagreements over what actually occurred normally were resolved in favor of the teacher or administrator. Undoubtedly, pedophiles were active in this environment and children were abused then just as they are today. Teachers, school administrators, parish priests, choir directors, and Cub Scout leaders abused children. But, as a whole, society tended to be in a mental state of denial. It refused to hear or see.

Following the conclusions of World War II and the Korean Conflict, representatives of a broader range of society began to use the GI Bill to earn college degrees and move into academic professions. Many of these persons opted for teaching. In response, liberal arts institutions began to expand, and the academic requirements for teaching certificates also began to expand. Many states moved from a minimum two-year degree to a four-year degree, and some began to require a fifth year.

Similarly, the professors staffing the teaching institutions during this period tended to have a broader and often more liberal view of the world and the teacher's place in it. Both the teachers and those who taught them began to organize into bargaining units and began to interact both professionally and as a labor organization on a national level.

By the 1950s, new teachers coming from liberal arts institutions tended to be a more assertive lot. They wanted higher incomes, improved job security, better working conditions, and respect for their Constitutional rights. But they also wanted to enjoy the historical "pillar of the community" status of the teacher. The rights and responsibilities of the public on the one hand, and teachers on the other, began to conflict. As the public paid more of its taxes to public education it tended to want more oversight and more respect for local, ethical, and moral values. As a result, civil rights litigation increased and teachers unionized, seeking additional protection in the form of collective bargaining agreements.

Shortly after the beginning of this educational revolution, administrator candidates began to emerge from this new breed of teachers, replacing their more traditional predecessors. In many respects, this new breed of administrator also became unionized and collective bargaining agreements between school districts and administrators became more common and even more complex.

But, this revolution was not uniform. In general, the economic benefits from teaching and the rights and protections teachers enjoyed tended to be greater in urban rather than rural areas. At the same time, the expectations of a mostly blue collar public were often radically different than the expectations of farmers. Therefore, one set of rights and responsibilities evolved for teachers and administrators in metropolitan areas and another for those in rural areas. Yet civil dismissal litigation involving small school districts, where the teaching staff might number twenty-five, for example, often dictated statewide consequences impacting school districts with teaching staffs in the hundreds. As a result, historical local standards came into conflict with the expanding legal and contractual rights and constitutional protections afforded to teachers in metropolitan areas. In order to protect the rights of the majority, the *statewide standard* began to become the norm.

Once the statewide standard was accepted, the legal ability of local school boards to impose local values on teaching staff suffered. Meanwhile, in order to impose the statewide standard on everyone, and, of necessity, to protect the rights of the rural and urban teachers, legislatures required local school boards to honor and enforce the statewide standard. During this period, traditional requirements imposed upon teachers, such as the requirement to reside in the employing school district, ceased to have any further force or effect.

While all of this was in play, the pedophile continued to be drawn to children; the game remained the same, the players remained the same, and only the rules were changing. Pedophiles continued to abuse and they continued to be caught. When they were caught they were dismissed from teaching. Everyone, including teachers, administrators, and the public supported that outcome. But a pedophile resisting his or her dismissal created legal precedent, and that legal precedent began to impact the existing rights of teachers in general. In particular, it became very difficult to distinguish between what degree of due process, constitutionally guaranteed, should be granted to a pedophile on the one hand, and how much should be afforded a teacher exercising his or her right to free speech on the other. The pedophile began to enjoy protections derived from free speech litigation and it became increasingly difficult to rid the profession of those who posed a clear danger to children. Neither labor nor management had desired this outcome, still, because no categorical legal distinction could clearly be made between the levels of due process which had to be provided, it became inevitable.

Eventually, even the distinction between due process afforded to a teacher being criticized for performance deficiencies in instructional skill and a teacher charged with sexual abuse of students began to break down, with both getting the same level of due process. Consequently, the pedophile found new defenses. In at least one case, a homosexual pedophile took classes, at his employing school district's expense, on how to identify the homosexual pedophile. He then used this new knowledge in order to avoid detection.

Through the 1970s teachers and school administrators, as a group, tended to deny there was a substantive problem. Whenever a pedophile would strike, get caught, and either admit error or find him or herself in a situation where denial was hopeless, this group would characterize the event as an exception within an otherwise exemplary profession that continued to deserve society's respect and deference. Usually, during this period, local education associations had rights and responsibilities committees of some sort, which would judge, on a case-by-case basis, whether or not the accused deserved a defense. These committees would summarily refuse the pedophile a defense, thus lining up with society against the child abuser. Like most checks and balances, once the pedophile denied guilt and insisted upon an equal right to representation, the local rights and responsibility committee concept failed. We ask, in this text, whose side should these committees be on?

A rights and responsibilities committee would be faced with the choice of either doing the right thing—denying services because the individual teacher's denial was found to be without merit—or doing the easy thing, treating this teacher the same as any other teacher who denied guilt. Frequently, when the committee did the "right thing," the education association was sued by the errant teacher for failing to provide "fair representation." The threat of these suits inevitably led the committees to favor the path of least resistance and, as a result, the pedophile would be given the same defense the teacher association provided to everyone else; or the errant teacher was "encouraged" to relocate and given a clean recommendation.

There would also be significant secondary considerations. Historically, teachers have insisted that they should not have to police their own ranks; that administrators and school boards have an absolute duty to remove those who should not be around kids. This philosophy has the dual benefit of providing a designated scapegoat in cases of obvious teacher failure and protects the teacher's association from the fracturing that inevitably occurs when one member or group is pitted against another. But, to use a cliché, it does not always "play well in Peoria." In particular, although they most often deny it, classroom teachers and administrators usually, at least, have suspicions and may often actually know who the pedophile is. Obviously, moving the teacher on without treatment did not benefit either the teacher or the teacher's future students. We therefore ask, is this the best solution?

Consistent with the foregoing approach, administrators have been inclined to use rationalizations to excuse their inaction. Some of these have their genesis in the liberal arts college curriculum studied by most administrators. For example, many administrators feel they have a constitutional duty to provide the suspect teacher with the benefit of the doubt. Some believe that the suspect employee must be treated as innocent until proven guilty and they usually also believe that it is someone else's responsibility to prove that guilt. The person or entity who must prove guilt varies. It may be the police, the prosecutor, the district attorney, the school board, or even the victim, but it is never the rationalizer. Many administrators cling to the belief that one complaint is insufficient, two do not necessarily form a pattern, and anonymous complaints should be discounted entirely. Faced with growing suspicions, some will convince themselves that only a written or in-person complaint is sufficient.

Many believe that because school staff are professionals, if the teacher is asked and denies inappropriate behavior, that is the end of it; the denial must be respected. Historically, this hear-no-evil, see-no-evil approach did have its day in the sun. But, the approach failed miserably and kids were hurt. The pedophile would be adjusting to his or her new conditions while the hurt being caused was so frequent and so pervasive that society could no longer ignore the problem by putting administrators and school directors in place who were tacitly encouraged to ignore it. Administrators are currently expected to ferret out the problem regardless of whether a formal complaint or an informal complaint was made. When there is no complaint, not even an anonymous call, society now expects the responsible school administrator to find and remove the pedophile.

Even so, society no longer trusts school administrators or teachers. Through its legislatures and courts, society first began to require close scrutiny of the teaching profession and of those put into daily contact with kids at school. Initially these efforts focused on the new hire, the person coming into contact with children for the first time. This approach assumed that those who were already there were good people who didn't deserve further scrutiny. But teachers who sexually abuse students (TSAS) kept cropping up. Some were closet pedophiles and some were not. In response, society insisted upon greater vetting of teachers and administrators. In response, pedophiles began to find new ways to get at children. They became bus drivers, grounds keepers, secretaries, custodians, and even unpaid volunteers or invited guests. In response, procedures for examination of support staff increased, and as it did, the financial burden of investigation also became greater. In response to these trends, the patron's negative attitude toward public education is beginning to pervade court opinions involving the due process protections afforded to teachers and administrators. Inherently harmful conduct now receives less due process than conduct that simply lacks educational purpose, which receives less due process than that applied to management criticism of instructional related deficiencies posing no health, safety, or welfare risks to students.

Currently, the primary focus is on degree of injury or anticipated adversity. Consequently, the state of mind or intent of the abuser is given less credence now. In many cases, the standard of proof as to state of mind is now that the perpetrator either knew or should have known the conduct was injurious. In some cases, the "deliberate indifference" standard is applied to an employee's action or failure to act. This is essentially a reckless conduct standard, which requires no particular state of mind at all. In the cases currently on the cusp of the law, deliberate indifference is presented as nothing more than gross negligence. Now the focus is on the rights of the victim, not the rights of the alleged perpetrator.

We are now on the verge of absolute responsibility for the health, safety, and welfare of all students. That is not only the students in Ms. Smith's room, but the students next door in Mr. Jones' room and the students in Mr. White's room in the adjoining school district in the adjoining town. Now the administrator who chooses not to see or hear is treated the same as the administrator who did see or hear but chose to do nothing. Now the law expects teachers and administrators to err on the side of reporting and acting rather than erring on the side of respecting the suspected employee's rights. We are approaching the era when we *all* share responsibility for *all* children as opposed to being responsible for only those in our immediate area of concern or classroom.

Currently, we are weighed down with overlapping legal and contractual standards, which have evolved over the past thirty years. Today the law often requires action against an employee while the collective bargaining agreement between the teachers or administrators and the school district tends to require ponderous delay or inaction. Routinely, there are two parallel due process systems, the legal one and the contractual one. The contractual system is commonly based upon the "just cause" test. This is a seven-part test, which includes no express consideration of student health, safety, and welfare. For example, it asks "Was the agency's investigation conducted fairly and objectively?" and "Was the degree of discipline administered by the agency in a particular case reasonably related to (a) the seriousness of the employee's proven offense and (b) the record of the employee in his or her service to the agency?" These are standards best suited to an automobile assembly line. Parents of children who may have been groomed or fondled by a teacher were not at the table when the collective bargaining agreement was made. They do not respect it and they do not respect management's reliance on it. They want action and they want it yesterday. Similarly, most collective bargaining agreements include a "progressive discipline" clause meaning that in most cases discipline is the least severe form not previously applied, e.g., warnings, then reprimand, then suspension, then dismissal. Again, we have an employee and union arguing the application of a collective bargaining agreement neither students or their parents ever agreed to. The resulting dissatisfaction is beginning to tear public education apart. Twenty-five states now allow some form of "independent" public schools that allow parents to do an end-run around these restrictive collective bargaining agreements.

The legal due process system often demands cessation of teacher–student contact as soon as possible risk is evident or foreseeable. State law generally looks at whether conduct is inherently harmful, the degree of adversity, the age and maturity of the students, and the likelihood of reoccurrence. State law generally insists action is required when *possible risk is foreseeable*. The system of contract rights generally requires "just cause," "progressive discipline," and ponderous due process systems that are either difficult or impossible to comply with. From a union viewpoint, the best due process system is one that cannot possibly work. This venue allows the teacher's association to blame retention on the administration.

Implementing administrators often do not know, or prefer not to acknowledge knowing, the difference between legal and contractual obligations. Routinely, teachers are allowed to "elect a remedy," meaning they are given the option to choose the due process system most favorable to them. Thus, while legislatures and courts establish tighter and tighter controls and expectations on teachers and school administrators (both public and private), the grievance-arbitration process routinely ignores these new standards and continues to apply outdated employee due process concepts from private industry to TSAS situations in schools.

Child abuse has been with us for as long as there have been children. Since children are dependent on adults for an extended period, they must be cared for, or uncared for, by those around them. As Radbill (1980) points out, children have generally been considered possessions with no rights of their own. Historically, infanticide was not only population control but also a desirable option in cases of deformed children

(Lynch, 1985). Clearly amniocentesis allows us to continue this practice. Children were always a cheap source of labor—in tribes, on farms, and in industrial factories. While these practices continue today throughout the world, they began raising the eyebrows of concerned professionals in the 17th century. The plight of children became of even greater concern in the early 20th century, giving rise to the child welfare movement. Concern for the humane treatment of animals in the 19th century was a harbinger of concern for children. Psychoanalysis added fuel to the fire when it convinced the educated public that early life events were the foundation of personality, and that sexual experiences were critical. Freud was not sure if abusive events actually occurred or were fantasized. (Interestingly, this controversy continues almost a hundred years later.)

The movement for the protection of children grew. In 1961 C. Henry Kempe made it known, unequivocally, that there was a "battered child syndrome." As civil rights became the most important domestic issue of the 1960s everyone's rights became scrutinized. Minorities, women, gays, and even children wanted to drink from the constitutional fountain. During the 1970s and 1980s the mental health marketplace expanded like a mushroom cloud. Counselors, therapists, social workers, psychologists, family therapists, and psychiatrists all needed to pay their overhead, justify their educational expenses, and fight for just causes. Child sexual abuse became a major battleground. As the feminist agenda strengthened and family values became a political rallying cry, the communists of the 1950s, the drug users of the 60s, and drunk drivers of the 1970s faded in the face of the public enemy number 1 of the 1980s and 1990s . . . the child sex offender. In this atmosphere,"innocent until proven guilty" became as ludicrous as when Senator Joe McCarthy accused someone of communist affiliations—it was a done deal. Like the historical communist, the sexual criminal became the bogeyman who threatened the very fabric of our so called decent society. An example of this excess is the "Violent Predator" Law in Washington State. Sex criminals can be held indefinitely, not for crimes they have committed and served sentences for, but for crimes they are likely to commit in the future. This is a far cry from the historical standard of "innocent until proven guilty. "

On top of this, the deterioration in the nuclear family (greater than fifty percent of biological parents will not raise their children) necessitates that more adults will be involved in children's lives. What are the roles of the teacher and school system? Are teachers being asked to relate to children in areas outside their training and beyond their job descriptions? Thus, as you begin to see, the issue of TSAS is an issue buffeted by many powerful societal pressures. We hope this book helps you to understand the problem and increases your sophistication in working with school personnel, students, parents, and the legal/criminal procedural mechanisms.

DR. STEPHEN RUBIN, PH.D.
Professor of Psychology
Whitman College
Walla Walla, Washington

JOHN S. BIGGS, J.D.
Attorney at Law
Lakebay, Washington

CHAPTER 2

Epidemiology: How Big Is the Problem?

BEFORE we offer a definitive answer, we need to define our terms: Sexual abuse is generally defined *legally* as any gender-based verbal or physical insult to one's sexuality. It can, however, also be defined more narrowly as only encompassing unwanted physical contact with one's erogenous zones. An adult sexually abuses a dependent, sexually immature child when the child is unable to fully comprehend and, thus, unable to give informed consent. Fraser defined child sexual abuse as the "exploitation of a child for the sexual gratification of an adult" (Fraser, 1981, p. 58). Similarly, Baker and Duncan said that "a child (anyone under 16 years) is sexually abused when another person, who is sexually mature, involves the child in any activity which the other person expects to lead to their sexual arousal" (Baker & Duncan, 1985, p. 458). The National Center of Child Abuse and Neglect defines child sexual abuse as "contacts or interactions between a child and an adult when the child is being used for the sexual stimulation of the adult or another person." Thus, it can be defined legally or socially. It can be viewed objectively or subjectively, e.g., if a person *feels* they have been abused, then they have been abused. Beginning in the 1980s and continuing since, the terms *child sexual abuse* and *sexual harassment* have begun to overlap and lose self-defining status. As Kempe and Kempe (1984) point out in *The Common Secret*, methods of gathering data lead to different estimates of abuse. Telephone surveys, reports from clinical practice, questionnaires distributed in schools, or reports from

13

governmental child protective services will all yield differing statistics.

At the beginnings of previous works on child sexual abuse, definitions and fine points are discussed, yet some commonalities remain. First, it is child sexual abuse if the victim is a child being used for sexual gratification by an adult or significantly older child. Second, it is sexual abuse if it is condemned by the society. For example, in the state of Washington, if the victim to consensual sexual contact is under the age of sixteen and the perpetrator is at least two years older, or the perpetrator is in a position of authority and at least five years older, *legally actionable* sexual abuse has probably occurred. Some states define the age of consent as age eighteen. In other societies, the Republic of France for example, the age of consent is thirteen.

According to Kempe and Kempe (1984), Judeo-Christian history is filled with incidents of child sexual abuse. Anal intercourse practiced on young boys by teachers and family members was acceptable in ancient Greece and Rome. Castration, circumcision, and clitorectomy have been performed for various reasons for thousands of years. Incest has occurred in all societies and was given special importance in the ruling families of Hawaii, some South American cultures, and some European and religious groups.

Incest is an important part of the teacher–student abuse syndrome. As we try to understand this problem we may compare it to other forms of abuse such as rape or intrafamily abuse, or molestation by a familiar adult figure such as the next door neighbor. Remember, we give our children to these trusted parent substitutes and then they defile that trust. They are generally not strangers.

An examination of child sexual abuse may begin with the historic view of children as little adults or as a possession of their parents (Haugaard and Reppucci, 1988). In 1922, English monarchs were given the obligation of defending the rights of children, idiots, and lunatics, who were incapable of defending themselves. States' rights have had to be balanced against the legal tradition of family privacy. In a strange irony the major block to elimination of incest may be the sanctity of the family—special privacy protections are afforded to the family and family values.

The label *child sexual abuse* first appeared in the Federal Child Abuse Prevention and Treatment Act of 1974, an act directed in part against incest. In 1970, the state of Florida had seventeen reports of child abuse, but in 1971, after a program of public education and implementation of a mandatory reporting law, there were 19,120 reports (Kempe and Kempe, 1984). In 1979, Edward Sarafina in the *Journal of Child Welfare* estimated that in a nation of 61 million children there were 74,725 reported cases of child sexual abuse and perhaps three to four times as many unreported cases. Thus, a decade ago, an expert estimated that there were perhaps as many as 336,000 cases of child sexual abuse in the United States each year.

The American Humane Society's Clearinghouse on Child Abuse estimated that between 60,000 and 100,000 children are abused each year (MacFarlane and Waterman, 1986). In retrospective surveys administered to college students, estimates of children's unwanted sexual contact with adults during their childhood range from 8–35% (MacFarlane and Waterman, 1986). Similarly, the Kempes (1984), reviewing several major studies, discussed rates of 4–19% for women and perhaps 8% for men. Russell (1983) did extensive interviewing of a non-clinical adult female population around San Francisco and found that if intrafamily and extrafamily incidents are combined, before age eighteen, then the incident figure for at least one such unwanted childhood experience is 38%! She also found that in her normal, non-clinical population only 2% of the intrafamily and 6% of the extrafamily abuse was ever reported.

The problem has been a real dilemma for psychologists for several reasons. Freud was uncertain whether adults' recollections about infantile and childhood sexual assaults were true. Were these memories actual accounts or fantasies? He concluded that either way these historical accounts were causative features of neurosis and sexual problems. Freud was not a family therapist. He worked with the adult victims of childhood sexual abuse. However, not all children are affected the same way. In 1976 (quoted in Russell, 1986) Wardell Pomeroy said, "Incest between adults and younger children can also prove to be a satisfying and enriching experience." In regard to these sorts of crosscurrents, therapists help people to explore their current psychological or emotional problems; and while society imposes a duty to report current child abuse, society generally fails to define to the therapists what historical events from an adult's past are reportable and what are not. This evidences a societal acknowledgement that the report itself is often potentially more damaging to the patient and family than the historical event itself may have been.

Are people as responsible for their abusive behavior if they themselves were abused? Currently, society's siren song is clear: Report them! Prosecute them! Lock them up! In *The Battle and the Backlash* D. Hechler (1988) reports that this law and order fever has led to a tremendous increase in allegations, but the substantiation index (proven cases) has remained fairly even at between 47–55%. This means that perhaps half the allegations are false or exaggerated.

Child abuse is often familial, occurring in a private setting with few if any corroborating witnesses and without tangible physical evidence. As a result, while it remains legally difficult to prove these sorts of cases beyond a reasonable doubt (the criminal law standard), all professionals in the field know that many of the worst cases occur in the midst of a familial child custody or dissolution case where there is no physical evidence of the abuse.

Also, children have a tendency to be difficult witnesses, often adopting the version of events proposed by the last influential adult they have interacted with. Elizabeth Loftus (1992, 1993), I. E. Hyman (1994), and Lee Coleman (1986, 1994) have all made names for themselves by demonstrating how memories can be created and how eyewitnesses may be wrong. But, in the process, they have also increased the protection of the true pedophile. As prosecution becomes more difficult, abusers not only avoid consequences, they also wrongfully gain an "innocent" determination, which allows them future access to children and opportunities for further abuse. The specific problem of sexual abuse of students by teachers is not even mentioned in the most recent important volumes on child sexual abuse.

Finklehor's *Child Sexual Abuse* (1984) and *A Sourcebook on Child Sexual Abuse* (1986), Kempe and Kempe's *The Common Secret* (1984), *The Sexual Abuse of Young Children* by MacFarlane and Waterman (1986), and *Sexual Crimes and Confrontations* by West (1987) all fail to discuss or even reference this important topic. Only in John Crewden's *By Silence Betrayed* (1988) is the topic described in a case example.

Similarly, in 1988 S. Rubin (author here) sent a questionnaire to the offices of education in all fifty states asking for information on the magnitude of this problem. The response was *underwhelming*. Twenty states did not respond at all. Twenty-one states sent brief apologetic letters with no data. Although this is a societal problem and has nothing to do with political boundaries, only nine states sent some data. In other words, only 18% of the state offices were willing or able to participate in the study. Clearly, this is an example of a profession that is failing to police itself.

The returned questionnaires showed that approximately seven to eleven cases of teacher–student sexual abuse per state per year were reported to the state level. Similarly, a telephone interview with California officials in 1988 determined that in 1979 there had been seventeen cases requiring mandatory certification revocation because of sexual acts. In 1982–83, the number had increased to twenty-nine and during the 1985–86 school year there had been fifty-two such cases. In five years there had been a 300% increase in incidents of teacher–student sexual abuse in California, but the numbers remained miniscule.

Thus, while experts on child sexual abuse are discussing hundreds of thousands or perhaps even millions of victims annually, school systems are admitting to (at most) several hundred cases nationally! In dealing effectively with teacher–student sexual abuse, the K–12 school system is not just an ostrich with its head in the sand, it is an ostrich which dons blinders and earplugs before putting its head in the sand. Similarly, *The Spokesman-Review,* a daily newspaper in Spokane, Washington, carried an exciting series on this problem in 1988. The paper had taken court action to successfully gain access to the incident files held by the state superintendent of public instruction. In this series, the paper asked women to look back through their childhoods for incidents of sexual abuse. Respondents reported 16% of the incidents involved teachers (3.3%—elementary level, 12.6%—secondary level).

A national survey of state teacher certification officials found that officials in twenty-seven states felt teacher–student sexual abuse incidents were increasing. A recent four-year study by Shakeshaft and Cohan (1995), based upon an inquiry to 764 school officials in New York State, of whom 43% responded, reported 192 claims of having dealt with staff–student abuse cases.

To give us some idea of the current incidence of sexual abuse cases within the educational system, the Office of Superintendent of Public Instruction of the state of Washington was contacted. In 1990, there were twenty-eight final actions of which twenty (71%) related to sexual abuse or inappropriate sexual behavior with students. Of the twenty, nineteen were male teachers, fourteen of the teachers had certificates revoked, and six voluntarily surrendered their certification. In 1991 there were eighty-six final actions taken of which sixteen were sexual in nature (18%). There was only one female teacher involved. Eleven licenses were revoked, three licenses were suspended, and two licenses were voluntarily surrendered. In 1992, there were 102 final actions and forty-nine of those (46%) were related to sexual issues. Two of the forty-nine were female. Nine licenses were revoked, twelve were voluntarily surrendered, four were suspended, two were reprimanded, and twenty-two cases were dismissed. In 1993, there were eighty-nine final actions of which twenty-eight (31%) were related to sexual misbehavior. There were six female and twenty-two male teachers involved. Six of the teachers had licenses revoked, three were suspended, seven voluntarily surrendered their licenses, and twelve cases were dismissed. In 1994, there were seventy-nine final actions of which twenty-three (29%) were sexual in nature. Two of the twenty-three were female, six cases ended in dismissal, nine voluntarily surrendered their licenses, five licenses were revoked, and three were reinstated.

Over the five-year span, from 1990 to 1994 only 136 cases of teachers sexually abusing students (TSAS) were investigated at the state level. Certainly there were many more accusations and local investigations. Interestingly, in the first half of the decade, we do not see a steady rise in cases. For some reason, 1992 was a year with many investigations but these involved only forty-nine cases of sexual misbehavior and twenty-two of those were eventually dismissed. If there are approximately 44,000 teachers in Washington State, the ratio of teachers charged to the overall number of teachers is approximately 0.6 to 1,000.

Similarly, in the Canadian publication, *The Alberta Journal of Educational Research* (1995), Dolmage found that there were .17 teachers charged per 1,000 teachers in the years 1987 through 1992. If only male teachers were studied, the ratio increased to .61 per 1,000. About 60% of the cases were withdrawn or ended with acquittals. Dolmage wrote this article partly to combat the popular myth that TSAS was a common phenomenon. His data indicates that, in fact, TSAS is not common and further, 50% of the cases were found not guilty.

Certainly, we can speculate about the reasons why experts do not include the teacher (and other school staff) offender in their works on child sexual abuse and why state officials do not acknowledge the problem. The fact that all teacher certification and state educational agencies are routinely staffed by former local school district staff and teachers may contribute to this educational community deafness. To even mention this area is to tiptoe around self-incrimination or at least, draw negative public attention to teachers. As a result, teacher associations (unions) at the national and state levels tend to discount the problem. Further, it is our belief that the topic creates a legitimate anxiety. Many teachers may have experienced feelings towards students and may have had close calls. As we discuss later, many are attracted to teaching because of a healthy attraction to students. This attraction is not unidimensional but complex. Few teachers are pedophiles. People do become teachers for many positive psychological reasons. In today's marketplace, teaching is a far from lucrative occupation so we must wonder what other factors influence this career choice.

CHAPTER 3

Case Studies

THIS chapter describes actual cases from our personal experiences. We will begin each case study with a description of the teacher, followed by a characterization of the victim(s), the interactions between them, and the outcome. Then we will present both psychological and legal analyses of the case.

ADULT MALES AND FEMALE STUDENTS

Case 1: Coach Joe and His Many Female Assistants

Joe was a middle-aged, married, junior high school basketball coach and science teacher. He had been teaching for approximately ten years, during which he had taught in three different states, serving in at least six different school districts. His wife was also a teacher.

The problem surfaced when his fourteen-year-old basketball team manager accused him of sexual misconduct with her. This had, in fact, progressed from kissing and fondling to eventual intercourse. At first, he denied the accusation, but eventually, he admitted misbehavior and sought assistance from the teacher's union. The school asked for his resignation. A "deal" was then made and he agreed to begin treatment. As a result of his cooperative attitude, Joe was not charged with criminal misconduct and therefore did not serve any jail time. Along the way, his wife decided to divorce him, and admitted to a relative that the problem was not new. Essentially the same conduct had occurred in state after state over a period of several years, and each time, Joe resigned and then found a new teaching position in another state. In each case, his record had failed to follow him to the new position. Along the way, he never actually sought treatment or admitted to either himself or his wife that he had a problem. The scenario always involved a special female student with whom he spent a lot of time. He was consistently seen as a dedicated, concerned, caring teacher/coach; one who was admired by his students' parents for his efforts.

Eventually, Joe left teaching and took a position managing a community recreation center, a position that allowed him to continue his involvement with athletics and young people. Some of his other jobs included being an assistant manager of a fast food restaurant and working for a state agency, where he first worked with the elderly but then asked to be transferred to a position where he would work with juveniles. His then ex-wife called the state office, informed them of Joe's past, and he was then dismissed. (Joe's wife's story is in the Appendix. Both she and their son are also victims.)

Psychological Analysis

Joe is a middle-aged man who remains fixated on his relationships to sports and to young women. His attraction to teaching is related to these fixations. His interest in athletics and pubescent (sic: young) females is a common and socially accepted fixation. Many models are teenagers and our country's interest in sports is obsessive. The amount of time and energy he devotes to teaching reveals his psychological addictions. His marriage suffers because of these addictions. The school system, parents, and students reward him because of his devotion. He cannot see the depth of his problem and sincerely believes, each time, it will not happen again. It is very difficult for him to consider or seek employment outside of the fields of youth athletics or, failing that, teaching. Thus, he does not see himself as a predator nor does he see any need for rehabilitative treatment. He fails to see the psychological trauma to his victims or his own family. His wife, who made a suicide attempt years before because of a similar situation, cannot report him or leave him.

Legal Analysis

.Joe's intent is not determinative. When dealing with sexual misconduct with students we do not have to prove a criminal or malicious intent. We need only consider that the misconduct lacks educational purpose, is inherently harmful, and that there is foreseeable risk if student–adult contact is maintained.

Joe is a classic example of why local education agencies must be required to report *suspected* abusers to state education agencies and why every state education agency should be integrated into a nationwide computer database. Every time Joe moved from one state to another, he should have been identified as a risk to kids. He was not, and that is the societal failure that permitted the problem to continue. Joe's ex-wife is not without fault here. She was society's watchdog. She knew what he was doing, and she knew the risk he posed. Eventually she acted to avoid further risk, but she should have done so much earlier. Her story is in the Appendix and, as that shows, she was a teacher herself. She had divided loyalties, both to Joe, their marriage and child, and to the school system. She knew though, for a long time, that Joe posed *a possible risk* to female students aged twelve to sixteen and rather than giving that class of persons the opportunity to avoid that risk, she chose to believe Joe.

Note that Joe was allowed to resign. Even so, he should have been discharged. He avoided that because he offered resignation and a school official chose to accept that resignation rather than pursue discharge. He should have been investigated and charged by police and prosecutors. A criminal record should have been developed and none was. In addition, every former school official who knew where Joe had gone and what he was doing had a duty to report his past to his new employer; this duty is not reactive, it is proactive. Children are children regardless of whether they live in Washington or California or New York and we all have a duty to protect them. That duty does not stop with the present and it does not stop with a state line.

Case 2: Nate, the "Natural Helper"

Nate was a thirty-one-year-old married high school teacher who coaches wrestling and junior varsity football and teaches communications. Nate was also the advisor to the "Natural Helper" program, which is a program that offers guidance to troubled students. Nate was married to a teacher and had two children. He was well-liked and popular with high school students. He had no criminal record.

Sherry, the victim, is an eighteen-year-old high school student with boyfriend problems, family problems, and physical difficulties. She went to Nate because he was faculty advisor to the Natural Helpers; she needed someone to talk to, and he was there for her. Sherry says that after talking to Nate about her problems, she became very attracted to him. The teacher would meet her, at night, at the community library. He would report to his wife that he was working late at school. Usually he would then take Sherry, in his vehicle, to an isolated location and have sexual intercourse with her. This occurred over a period of four months. Eventually, she reports having had intercourse in Nate's vehicle on several occasions, and once on the stage at the high school after hours.

Nate broke off the relationship with Sherry, claiming a religious objection. Six months later, Sherry told a girlfriend about the affair and the girlfriend then reported it to a female staff person at the high school. Nate adamantly denied the charges. Both were then asked to take a polygraph. Sherry took and passed the polygraph. Nate refused. At the end of the school year, Nate resigned his position and pursued a new career in radio journalism.

Psychological Analysis

Sherry was an attractive, psychologically needy teenager who was drawn to a teacher because of her need to talk about her problems. This teacher enjoyed the intimate conversation and feeling of doing well as a Natural Helper. An untrained and unsophisticated lay counselor, he did not understand how the combination of his needs and what is called the *transference relationship* could lead to sexual involvement. Professional therapists recognize that their feelings for patients and the patients' feelings for them are deeper and only indirectly due to personal characteristics. The intimacy of talking about problems in an isolated after-hours environment can easily become sexualized. The marketplace of counseling has become populated by many people who should not be involved in helping others. Lay counselors "Natural Helpers," even school counselors should not be in the mental health business. They lack the education and understanding necessary to be of assistance without becoming entangled in the problems of their needy clients. A supervisor or trained therapist might help the lay counselors realize when they need to refer the "hurting person" to a fully trained therapist. In this case, the naive, poorly or untrained staff doesn't recognize Sherry's or Nate's needs.

From my national survey I found that coaches and counselors are the types of school personnel who are likely to be sexually involved with students. Likewise it is students who are having trouble, who have low self-esteem, who are in need of someone to make them feel worthwhile, and those who have a precocious or active sexuality who are the most likely to be involved with teachers. This is a classic match-up. These situations must be acknowledged by school systems, discussed, and ultimately controlled and avoided.

Legal Analysis

This was a case wherein the popular and personable teacher was allowed, as a defense, to attack the girl from the other side of the tracks. For example, Sherry, early on, had told her boyfriend that she had sex with the teacher once; later, she claimed several encounters, both in his vehicle and at school. As a result of the earlier declaration to the boyfriend, she was attacked as a liar. This led, in part, to the administration's insistence on a polygraph of the victim. Even when she passed the test, the administration chose not to address whether or not Nate "posed a risk to the health, safety, and welfare of students." Instead, the administration insisted on reframing the question as, "Do we have enough evidence to prove a dismissal?" Those *are not* the same questions.

Nate was not dismissed. Instead, he was eased out of teaching and the investigation was referred to the state education agency for consideration of certificate revocation—an unlikely outcome since no adverse action notice had been issued by the local education agency. In the process, the student-victim was not well supported by the school, and Nate was left in a position to hurt others in the future.

This situation also raises serious legal concerns about the "Natural Helpers" program. Did Nate's involvement in that program either cause or contribute to an injury to Sherry? That can be considered a question-of-fact which may be allowed to go to a jury. Also, in general, schools are not responsible for protecting students from injurious activities of fellow students, but schools are responsible for protecting students from injurious activities by staff persons. Here, an untrained lay counselor has been put in a position where a student has been disadvantaged. That is the sort of mix that breeds lawsuits.

Point–Counterpoint

Psychologist: I believe that Nate should be allowed to continue as a teacher unless there is evidence that he is incompetent. He is not a pedophile and there is no history of him as a child molester. This appears to be a first sexual situation with a student and he was unaware of the deeper psychological forces at play. He needs to give up counseling students and focus on his teaching duties. He needs counseling to help him understand underlying problems in his marriage and areas of disturbance in his own cognitive/moral make-up. A suspension with treatment, ongoing treatment, and restrictions as to his teaching duties all seem to be good conditions to impose. I do not believe that Nate is a great danger to other students if he receives competent therapy.

Also, it seems to me that the school system needs to carefully consider programs such as "Natural Helpers." Programs under the auspices of a school system must be carefully planned and watched. Pitfalls such as the relationship between Nate and Sherry are predictable and procedures eliminating them or monitoring them can be built into the programs. These are not one in a million totally unexpected cases. Helping people in need is risky business.

Attorney: In my opinion keeping Nate as a teacher is not an option, student contract poses a danger. There is a foreseeable risk. Certainly, this risk can be ·minimized and Professor Rubin's suggestions, "A suspension with treatment, ongoing treatment, and restrictions as to his teaching duties all seem to be good conditions to impose. I do not believe that Nate is a great danger to offend against other students if he receives competent therapy." seem to me to be akin to suggesting that being a little bit pregnant is somehow different than being a lot pregnant. I do not agree. Nate is a risk and suspending him and treating him is proof of that. I do not believe we should defer to any sort of employee rights or contract rights once we have reached the conclusion that a teacher has engaged in inherently harmful conduct without educational purpose. But, I hasten to add that Dr. Rubin's solution is exactly the solution adopted later by the state education agency. Nate was allowed to keep his teaching certificate . . . he may be your teenage daughter's high school teacher today.

Case 3: Josh, the Seventh-Grade Science Teacher

Josh was a forty-three-year-old married science-math teacher in a middle school. He had taught for about twenty years. He had no criminal history involving sexual misconduct and no history of psychological treatment.

In 1993 there were allegations of inappropriate touching of female students' buttocks, looking at girls' bottoms when they were at the pencil sharpener, tickling girls under the arms, putting hands on girls' shoulders, looking down girls' blouses, looking up girls' skirts, and making female students feel uncomfortable. Josh denied the allegations. A notice was issued to Josh describing the allegations and his denial, but no treatment was directed and no reassignment to another grade level or other work adjustment was made. When the allegations were made, Josh had insisted on knowing the girls' names, and that request was denied. During the previous school year, students believed that much the same sort of misconduct had occurred, but follow-up interviewing regarding students' allegations failed to confirm this.

Earlier, in 1989, Josh had a new principal and there was a new series of complaints. Ten to twelve students complained and were interviewed. The superintendent issued a letter to Josh indicating that Josh is treating girls differently than boys, that Josh is putting his hand on girls' shoulders while they are working, the girls report feeling "uncomfortable" around him, and they worry that when he is standing above and behind them he may be looking down their shirts. Some girls reported being touched or tickled and being made to feel uncomfortable from that. Josh was directed to "be careful to avoid touching and tickling and to be careful to treat boys and girls the same." Otherwise, no warning or reprimand was given. In fact, the letter says, "I do not intend this letter to be any sort of reprimand," and went on to say, "We investigated this matter and found no evidence that anything improper had occurred." Josh was returned to the same classroom at the same grade level in the same building.

In 1990, there were new complaints. A female student reported extreme discomfort. "She was uncomfortable with the attention and personal comments you direct to her, especially remarks about beautiful eyes or beautiful hair." Josh was advised to "limit your contact with students during non-instructional time, for example, during lunch and non-school-related evening activities."

In 1992, there was a parent complaint that Josh had encouraged girls to eat lunch with him, had bothered one girl in particular about going square dancing in the evenings with him and offers to take her to and from the dance, which was several miles away. One girl had said many times she was feeling uncomfortable around him, and he had invited two girls to call him on a Saturday if they went to a school cleanup, and he would take them to lunch. All these activities are viewed by the school as contrary to the 1990 notice advising Josh to avoid non-instructional contacts with students. A comprehensive investigation was begun. This investigation revealed that Josh had met and groomed his first wife when she was thirteen years of age, by inviting her to square dancing practices. By age fourteen they were "going steady," and they were married when she was seventeen. She recalled Josh telling her about his having visited two ten-year-old twin girls, sitting between them on a couch and fondling both under a blanket over their laps. She recalled him reporting doing much the same thing with a twelve-year-old. She reported he had sexual difficulties with intercourse and had a great need to control her. She recalled that he always had little girls around and was constantly talking about these girls. He was always trying to get young girls involved in square dancing or in his after-school rocket club. She said, "I was convinced he was sexually attracted to young girls."

Immediately prior to this latest complaint, Josh was continuing to invite female students into his classroom during lunch for "games." This game had to do with them lying down and him using a puzzle to unbutton a blouse or to imagine their skin was "being unzipped." This occurred in an isolated portable classroom. He also sent pictures and notes to students inviting them to square dancing and gave students personal presents.

Some fifty students were interviewed and various incidents of the sort described above were identified and confirmed. Josh was issued a notice of dismissal. He did not resist the notice. A copy of the school's investigation was sent on to the state education agency and, as a result, Josh lost his teaching certificate.

Psychological Analysis

Josh is psychologically disturbed. From the evidence of his first wife's description of their marriage, through the feelings of uncomfortableness of his students over a period of several years, to the little games he played with his sixth- and seventh-grade students, it is evident that he has serious sexual problems. He is warned by school officials to curtail his non-classroom activities but he cannot resist, and repeats. He denies any inappropriateness and his denial precludes his seeking professional help. This denial, given the overwhelming evidence, suggests even more the seriousness of his problems. He appears to be obsessed with little girls, and though there is no evidence of direct sexual contact, these girls clearly are picking up on Josh's feelings.

There is an immaturity to Josh. He does not appear to have the mature sexuality of a person who will act out his fantasies.

He is inhibited in his direct expression of his sexual needs but it is uncertain what he is capable of. He cannot totally control his sexuality and consequently he puts his students in jeopardy. It is his persistence, year after year, which demonstrates his sexual compulsiveness. His wife's description of his private sexuality coupled with his ongoing behavior with his young students is convincing evidence of serious sexual problems which the school system, especially during the 1990s, must address.

Legal Analysis

Josh was defended so well he lost his job. A "warning" is notice and Josh was given notice in 1988 and 1989 and 1990. Well before 1992, Josh should have been in treatment, and his union representative's support of his denials of culpability allowed him to avoid dealing with his psychological disability. Could he have been cured? I doubt it very much. But he could have been moved to high school where he would have been away from the particular age group he focused on. Students at the high school level are more mature and better able to handle this sort of unwanted attention.

Josh should have been discharged or, at least, given a reprimand the first time the inappropriate touching and attention occurred. In 1988, he was touching girls in a way that lacked educational purpose and was inherently harmful. There was no legal need to give him only a formal warning not to do that. Society presumes we know not to do certain things. We do not allow defense for rape or murder, for example, by a claim that no one said not to do that. The second time Josh offended, which was in 1989, he should have been dismissed. By 1990, he was overdue. By 1992, every victim he encountered from 1989 on was an unnecessary one. Every one of them had a lawsuit against the school.

Point–Counterpoint

Psychologist: Josh is not a rapist. There is not overwhelming evidence that he is a child molester. He clearly demonstrates sexual problems, which are in need of treatment. Treatment should have been demanded by the school system in 1988 as well as the suggested behavioral restrictions: At that time, Josh could have been maintained as a classroom teacher.

Attorney: I expect school officials evaluated the 1988 situation by asking whether they had sufficient cause to dismiss, and deciding they did not, they then elected to do almost nothing. That is the wrong approach. Kids were being hurt and instead of deferring to employment rights, they should have either dismissed Josh or put him in an assignment where he had nothing whatsoever to do with sixth- and seventh-grade girls. Essentially, Dr. Rubin proposes to use those students as tools in Josh's rehabilitation and he presumes rehabilitation is achievable with little or no risk to those students. To me, any risk is unacceptable and society has no duty to put its children in harm's way in order to possibly allow a dangerous teacher to become less so.

Psychologist: Seeing the children as "a tool" for Josh's rehabilitation is incorrect. In 1988 there seemed to have been much doubt about Josh's dangerousness. There will always be some teachers who make some students feel uncomfortable. It would be an impossible witch hunt to eliminate all lascivious teachers from the education environment. We would worry about anyone who would be left.

Case 4: What about Bob? A Teacher–Student Love Affair

The majority of TSAS cases involve a male teacher and a female student. Within this general category however, there are several subsets. The following is an example of the most common category, the female high school student and the male teacher.

Bob was a high school science teacher. He also had an extracurricular assignment as girls' softball coach. As science teacher, he had a student teaching assistant, Susan, who also played on the softball team. Bob became a personal friend to Susan, working with her after practice. They discussed her athletic abilities and her plans for the future. Over time, their conversations became more personal and more intimate. They began to talk about each other. About this time, there was rumor that Coach Bob's assistant, Al (a fellow teacher), and another female student, Gail, had more than a student–coach relationship. No investigation of that rumor took place.

Physical contact between Bob and Susan began to increase. Susan later said that Bob frequently used the pretext of demonstrating softball skills to touch and hold her. On team bus trips, Susan and Bob would privately hold hands. When Susan became Bob's teacher assistant, her contacts with Bob at school increased. Susan also became Bob's student coaching assistant, working with the freshman female athletes. At this time, Bob was called in by his principal and asked if he was involved with Susan. Bob denied the involvement. Thereafter, the principal also separately interviewed Susan, who also denied the involvement. As a result, no further investigation took place at that time.

More and more, in school, Bob found ways to touch Susan's legs or to put his hands under her clothes.

Although Bob was married, toward the end of her junior year, Susan and Bob made an arrangement to meet at a journalism class party held at another teacher's house. Both made separate excuses to leave the party and met to pet and engage in intercourse.

During the summer between Susan's junior and senior year in high school, she and Bob had sex two or three times per week, usually in deserted areas of parks around the city where they lived. Bob and Susan's sexual relationship continued through her senior year in high school. Most of their contacts took place in Bob's car. Later, he got a van.

Susan began to pull away from her relationships with her peers and focused more and more on Bob. She accused her friends of trying to undermine their relationship. Occasionally, Susan would call Bob at his home.

Toward the end of her senior year, Susan and Bob were occasionally late getting in. On a couple of occasions, they were together until about 11:00 P.M., ostensibly following a late softball practice. The disputes between Susan and her parents increased to the extent that she finally moved in with her brother. In the spring of her senior year, Bob convinced his wife Helen that Susan was in trouble and needed a place to stay and that she could help him and Helen out with their children. Bob then moved Susan into his own house.

While living in the home, Susan believed that Bob's wife had actually seen them having sexual contact. The relationship continued for several months until Susan found a note from Bob to another female high school student. Susan became distraught and Bob gave her antidepressants. Susan eventually made a suicide attempt. At the hospital, she told her story and the authorities became involved. Later, both Susan and her parents brought a civil suit against Bob and the school system.

Susan had a long history of difficulties with her parents, especially her mother, although there is some evidence that her father struck her on occasion. Apparently, because the home was dysfunctional, her brother left home immediately upon graduation from high school.

Susan was quite thin. A female coach had commented, to the entire girl's basketball team, that Susan was anorexic. Susan was devastated by this experience and distracted by it.

Susan was a participant at a party where alcoholic beverages were consumed. Both male and female athletes were present and when the incident became known, Susan and several others received a five-day suspension from school. Her fellow students' knowing about this devastated her.

Susan had not dated a lot. In her freshman year, she had two dates and her parents insisted on meeting both boys who took her out. In her sophomore year, she was not allowed to go to drive-in movies and had a midnight curfew. These restrictions were a bit more restrictive than those imposed on other students her age.

Psychological Analysis

Susan was a disturbed and psychologically needy young person. Her anorexia suggested problems with her family, a feeling of inadequacy, difficulties with sexuality, and control issues. The attention that Bob gives her is well received. Her parents restricted her dating and it is possible that she felt that they were treating her like a little girl. Bob's interest in Susan satisfied many psychological needs. She feels mature, wanted, and may fantasize that Bob is going to leave his family and marry her. Eventually Bob kisses Susan and makes her feel co-responsible, saying "you knew that it was wrong before you did it." This projection of responsibility is often done by child molesters and increases the likelihood that the victim will keep the secret. Bob convinces Susan that his marriage is crumbling and that their love is justified. By the time Susan acquiesces to intercourse she believes that she is responsible for her actions. Following the intercourse, Susan readjusts her thinking to further ease remaining emotional doubts and emotional pain. This is dissonance reduction and it occurs after many difficult decisions.

Bob is the typical aging athlete dealing with marital problems and questions about his own vitality. He relates to adolescents differently than other teachers. His love of sports and continued involvement permits him to appear youthful rather than from an older generation. His athleticism makes it appear that he is still out there playing and not growing old. This is not true of all middle-aged athletes, but my 1988 research found that coaches are the most common TSAS. These men tend to be very controlling. That is why we call them "coach." Other non-coaching teachers also tend to have control issues with students and wives.

As it eventually came out in the defense, there had been rumors in the school system for some time of other teacher–student trysts. It is not certain whether Bob groomed Susan but the progression of contact followed the typical pattern. The distance between Susan and her parents increased as did the distance between Susan and her peers. Bob's wife chose not to intervene and it is uncertain how much discussion went on between them about Susan.

As the relationship continued, Susan became more respectable as a young woman. Where did her responsibility begin? Psychologically, could she have chosen to continue a relationship with an older married man? Her psychological instability is evidenced by her eventual suicide attempt. Bob's problems are clearly highlighted by moving Susan into his house and his feeding her antidepressant medications. This is way beyond a flirtatious affair. Because of the teacher's involvement, Susan was developing abnormally in her relationships to her parents and age-appropriate males. These problems began before Bob, but were magnified by his use of Susan. He seems totally unconcerned with the damage he is causing this student. His note to another student demonstrates his sexual appetite and his disregard for student welfare.

Legal Analysis

Note that we come to that point in time when the principal has a conversation with Bob about an allegation. Then, the principal met with Susan and, relying upon her denial, had a follow-up meeting with Bob in which he was "more conciliatory." That told Bob he was enjoying ultimate success. In particular, the principal's reaction to Susan told Bob that Susan had denied inappropriate behavior; later, when Susan became more forthright, the earlier denial would be raised as proof that she was not credible and should not be believed. The principal's "conciliatory" reaction told Bob that the principal had been compromised too. Very simply, a principal who holds meetings of this sort and then does nothing is not inclined to later see or hear the proof that he or she was previously wrong to desist from further inquiry. Many administrators caught in this dilemma will later become unintentionally obstructive to anyone attempting to revisit the question of whether or not an inappropriate teacher–student relationship had existed on their watch.

Note that Susan had begun to pull away from her peers and focus on her relationship with Bob. This made her student friends and associates suspicious. Investigation will show that they tried to learn from Susan what she was thinking and what she was doing, and when they were unsuccessful, they talked among themselves. Investigation will usually show that Susan and Bob were not as successful as they thought they were; other students saw the certain smile, the look, the touch. They knew enough to satisfy themselves that there was an affair, and they knew enough to purposely not look further. Why? If an affair were found, it would be reported. They would then become involved in a situation they could not control.

In my experience, as a general rule, teachers like Bob sexually abuse several Susans. Very simply, Susans grow up and as they mature, teachers like Bob begin to groom new Susans in younger grades; thus, the note from Bob to another female high school student—the next Susan being groomed. In one case I investigated, a male shop teacher had, over a period of years, seven "teaching assistants." He inappropriately touched six, had sexual contact with three of the six, and intercourse with two of them. He did that in a small town high school with fewer than 250 students.

When the last "teaching assistant" complained, the school administrators and fellow teachers denied that they had seen any of it. That is nonsense. They did not see or hear because they did not want to see or hear. In situations of this sort, administrators must be required to recognize that Susan, a student in high school, was there to fulfill the prescribed requirements to earn a high school diploma; she wasn't there to be a softball player or a teaching assistant. Both those roles exposed Susan to a more familial relationship with her coach or teacher and thus, required increased administrator vigilance to ensure that the teacher was not violating his fiduciary or trust relationship by taking advantage. Here, the administrators failed to recognize that there will always be a Susan and there will always be a Bob, and when we allow extraordinary contact between teachers and students associated with extracurricular activities, such as sports and assistantships, a strict additional scrutiny must go with it.

There is no defense for this behavior. The teacher–student relationship is historically well-defined. It does not include personal and intimate conversations. It does not include hand holding. It does not include out-of-school, personal, one-on-one contact. There is no need to wait until sexual gratification is suspected or proven; when a relationship that has no educational purpose is apparent, it is time to act.

In this case, there were rumors about female students' involvement with other male teachers. These were rumors of associations other than that between Bob and Susan. Later, when the lawsuits were in play, Susan and her parents successfully argued to a jury that even though she and Bob had been called in and had denied involvement, if the school had investigated those other associations at an earlier point in time, Bob never would have had an opportunity to groom her to begin with. The claim was that the educational environment was permissive, that it condoned these sorts of liaisons. The argument was innovative because the state did not allow a cause of action for "negligent investigation" but Susan's theory was allowed to go to a jury anyway, and it was successful.

Point–Counterpoint

Psychologist: Who is responsible for this long-enduring affair? Clearly, Bob is at fault. He has clearly gone outside the baselines of the ball field and the classroom as well as marriage. The school system is responsible for the atmosphere pervading student–teacher relations and their inadequate investigation early on. I contend that Bob's wife, Susan's parents, and Susan are also responsible. Bob is not the only bad guy. As a psychologist exploring how these affairs happen there seems to me to be many factors rather than just big bad Bob. If we are to really address these situations we need to see the complexities. Susan is a maturing young woman with self-esteem needs, identity needs, and sexual needs. Her parents and her community, including her school system, are the air she breathes. They are there to guide her and, at times, question her. Friends can and should be helpful. All of these correctional devices failed. Bob was allowed to be the powerful influence going almost unchecked. Even his wife is unwilling or unable to dissuade him when he moves Susan into their home. Clearly this affair of several years' duration goes too far. It seems psychologically impossible for Susan's parents to accept some guilt, but I feel that they must. At what point do we absolve parents of their responsibilities? Also, if women are to become equal partners in our society, and if child criminals are to be charged as adults, we must see sixteen- to eighteen-year-old females as at least partially responsible for what bed they lie in. I am not eliminating Bob as the major culprit. He should be removed from teaching and charged with statutory rape, but others are also at fault.

Attorney: Dr. Rubin's point about shared responsibility did later find its way into the civil trials. The "comparative negligence" concept was applied and because the jury found, in fact, that they did share responsibility, both Susan and her parent's claims were discounted to reflect that shared responsibility. With regard to the duration of the affair and the time when Susan evolved from immature adolescent to adult, as a society, we use several benchmarks. First, we generally do not allow adolescents to share responsibility until they reach at least the age of fourteen and we then increase that responsibility as they mature. With regard to sexual liaisons, the state of Washington defines the age of consent as sixteen; other states define it as eighteen. But we do not apply the same standard to teachers. When a teacher in the state of Washington has a sexual relationship with a person of student age, that is considered unprofessional conduct.

Here, Bob's conduct was unprofessional. In Washington, we require that any local school district superintendent must report reasonable cause to believe that a certificated staff person is not of good moral character or has engaged in acts of unprofessional conduct. The report is due to the state educational agency. Failure to report is in itself unprofessional conduct that exposes the local district super-intendent to loss of certificate.

Together though, as this case confirms, these various concepts do not fully protect. In public schools, we deal with the educational environment and exercise best efforts to avoid invading the privacy of the habitation or family environment. But here you see a case where the proof of an inherently harmful teacher–student relationship was in the home, not at school. Similarly, applying the age sixteen benchmark to sexual consent does not work, because Susan was still a student and Bob was still a teacher. Therefore, as a practical matter, in Washington, the age of consent for sexual intercourse between a teacher and student begins when the student ceases to be a student at graduation or release from school, plus reaching the age of consent.

It is easy to blame the school system and certainly some blame is due. But, administrators are not trained investigators and the school system is not a twenty-four hour a day system. As long as there are male teachers like Bob and emotionally needy female students like Susan, either these cases will recur or we must radically reform our educational system to ensure they cannot re-occur.

Case 5: Down on the Farm with Fred, the FFA Advisor: a Male Teacher Obsessed with Teenage Girls

When he first came to our attention, Fred was about twenty-five years of age. He was finishing his second year of teaching. He was the vocational-agricultural teacher in a very small Western school district, which comprised a total of about 125 students, grades K–12. Fred had grown up on a Western cattle ranch. He had done some rodeoing and had also raised wheat and barley and peas. In addition, Fred was a good metal shop teacher who had done his share of welding and metal cutting while growing up on the farm and who knew how to maintain farm equipment. The farmers in the area all liked Fred and hoped he would stay around awhile. Many of the local ranchers, especially those with daughters, had noticed that Fred was single.

In addition to being the vocational-agricultural teacher, Fred was also the Future Farmers of America (FFA) advisor. In this capacity, he assisted students in preparing farming exhibits, projects, and animals for show. He acted as student chaperone for local fairs and agricultural events, where the students routinely stayed overnight to care for their livestock. Fred was also the girl's basketball coach. He had played basketball in high school and college and knew the game well. Fred seemed to be emotionally immature. He had no adult friends. The other teachers did not invite him into their social groups and he would attempt to interact socially with the kids. In particular, he would get involved with them in pick-up basketball games at the school gym on weekends. When he was at a fair or agricultural outing with them, he would often "hang out" with the kids rather than with the adults. The girl's team had definitely improved since he took over as coach. To the local patrons, Fred's idiosyncrasies did not seem all that bad. In a small town, being a winning coach overcomes a lot of other perceived, or even real, disabilities.

When Fred first came to our attention, he had been on an FFA "home visit" to the farm operated by Amy and her family. Amy was one of his students, then aged fourteen. During this visit, Amy's father had encountered her and Fred in the barn where they were hugging and kissing. Amy's dad didn't see the educational purpose in that activity and complained about it to the principal, who then began an investigation. The investigation revealed that Amy had welcomed the hugging and that Amy had initiated the kissing. The investigation also revealed that Amy's mom was not of the same mind as her dad, the mom suggesting that the school ought "to mind its own business" and leave Amy and Fred to theirs. She noted that Fred was single, that Amy was too, and there were worse things than seeing Fred and Amy end up together.

During this investigation, which involved interviews of three female students and three of the twelve teachers on the teaching staff, it became apparent that Fred had some other failings. As girl's basketball coach, he had recently inadvertently wandered into the girl's locker room without warning, encountering several of his female players in states of partial, or in some cases, total undress. But, the moms interviewed reported that there was no indication that Fred had done this intentionally and, besides, the team was winning. No complaint had been made about this. Also, in the course of his coaching, Fred had exhibited a tendency to put his arm around players at times, in some cases draping his hand over a breast. In addition, while on outings with his students to a county fair and a tractor exhibition, Fred had been seen tickling the girls under their arms and engaging in frontal hugging with female students. When interviewed later, one girl complained that Fred had repeatedly brushed his shoulder and upper arm against her breast. The girls talked among themselves about this but none of them told their parents about it or complained to any school official about it. Again, Fred was a good coach, the girl's team was winning, and each of these girls was on the team.

Fred was confronted with this information and readily admitted that he had hugged and kissed Amy, that he knew it "probably weren't right," but he'd done it anyway. He admitted he wandered into the girl's locker room while he was distracted. He admitted "puttin' my hands where they don't belong." He whined and he cried, and he asked for another chance. He promised he would never do "nothin' dumb like that again."

The superintendent was not amused and he was inclined to summarily dismiss Fred but, recalling whom he worked for, he chose to consult his school board. The board was made up of five local men and women from the agricultural community who advised firm, but restrained, discipline. Fred was given a reprimand. He was admonished to avoid out-of-school contact with his students, especially the female students. He was pointedly told that if he continued to inappropriately touch students, regardless of intent, or wandered into the girl's locker room again, for whatever reason, he would be dismissed. Fred was required to undergo a regime of therapeutic counseling with a clinical psychologist intended to train him in how to appropriately interact with female students. Fred readily agreed to all these conditions and the reprimand. He apologized and seemed to have learned a hard lesson. Perhaps, if Fred had not been such a good vocational-agriculture teacher and if the girl's basketball team hadn't been winning, he might have been dismissed. However, there was no support for that solution among the local farmers who made up the school board.

Three school years later, there was a new complaint involving a student who had not been involved earlier. This time, while on a "home visit" to Jan's farm, Fred had been sitting on the porch swing with Jan when he playfully grabbed her, tickled her under the arms, and proceeded to lift her up and sit her on his lap—all activities having been observed by Jan's dad, who like Amy's dad a few years earlier, saw no educational purpose to any of this and promptly ran Fred off the farm. Jan was then fourteen. She had not enjoyed being pawed by Fred; she was upset by what Fred had done and doubly upset by her dad's anger. The superintendent was contacted and a new investigation was begun.

In retrospect, in the three years since the earlier investigation, Fred had not learned a thing. This time six female students, seven moms, and three dads were interviewed along with three teachers. Several girls had been fondled and had been offended. One girl had not been offended and rumors were that this girl had repeatedly engaged in sexual intercourse with Fred. All the girls involved had been associated with Fred as their supervisor either through his vocational-agricultural teaching, his FFA activities, or his coaching of girl's basketball and, in some cases, all three at the same time.

During the time between the conclusion of the first investigation and the beginning of the second, Fred had married and he and his wife had separated. The estranged wife was contacted and readily agreed to be interviewed about Fred's activities. She indicated that the reason for the breakup had been Fred's "obsession with teenage girls." Apparently Fred had even brought one of the girls home and the estranged wife believed he had engaged in acts of sexual intercourse with this student in the spousal bed. She was divorcing him and believed he should be dismissed. She also had some other suggestions as to appropriate penalty, one of which involved the involuntary removal of certain body parts without anesthesia.

A notice of dismissal was issued. This time, the local education association referred Fred to a psychologist who reported back to the union that Fred should not be allowed around teenage girls. The union then promptly proposed a settlement whereby Fred would voluntarily give up his teaching certificate to the state certification authority and voluntarily resign at mid-year. The school district, in return, agreed to withdraw the dismissal. Fred then left the district to go into partnership with his parents as a cattle rancher. Fred was not prosecuted and no student ever came forward to admit to intercourse or make civil complaints against Fred or the school district based upon Fred's previous activities.

Psychological Analysis

The demographic risk factors delineated at the beginning of this case raise concerns. Fred was young, single, a coach, and a teacher who spent much of his time after hours away from the school setting. His social relationships were with his students, not his colleagues. He seemed emotionally immature. There is a tendency for some athletic persons to "fixate" or remain youthful. While, as a society, we generally consider this a positive attribute, it is also a risk factor for a teacher when relating to younger students. Fred's idiosyncrasies and his youthfulness were accepted partly because of his success as a coach. Many times we have seen how coaches and athletes are coddled or treated as special because of how much we value athletics. Perhaps it is time for schools to reconsider the priority given to athletics.

When the initial investigation was made, the principal concluded that Amy had initiated the hugging and kissing. But, so what? The law says a student below a specified age, typically sixteen or eighteen, cannot consent. Therefore, the teacher was in the wrong regardless of whether the student initiated the amorous activity or the teacher did. Also, just because Amy's mother did not object to Fred's activities with her daughter, it does not necessarily follow that the school should not object.

Fred's other minor misbehaviors begin to suggest a pattern or at least a sexual inclination towards young girls. Fred's promise that he would not do it again should not have been accepted as the last word. Sex offenders and criminals make many sincere promises and while it is preferable that they do, as a society we need to insist upon more. That is what the school board required here. As a psychologist, I agree with the recommendations they made. I may have added to the chaperone and situational controls, but in general agreed with the school's first reaction. But, three years later, new charges were heard.

These new charges were more serious and clearly were in opposition to his earlier reprimand. The earlier controls placed on his activities had failed to prevent reoccurrence. We do not know the substance of the counseling sessions that took place prior to the reoffense. We do know that his marriage failed and we know that his ex-wife believed him to have been fascinated with teenage girls.

The school system dismissed Fred and let him quietly go out to pasture. I wonder if his compulsion continues to this day. He was not prosecuted for what may have been "rape of a child." While such a prosecution might have brought new psychological damage to his victim(s) and negative publicity to the school system, it might have justly punished Fred and also forced him to live the rest of his years under the sex offender regulations of the state. This case thus demonstrates how a well-meaning school board tried to deal with a beginning teacher with a strong sexual attraction for underage females. Clearly, the board members did not realize the power of his compulsion; Fred, even after having been caught, could not avoid reoffending.

Legal Analysis

In retrospect, the first investigation had too narrow a focus. In particular, it focused on whether there had been hugging and kissing between Fred and Amy, and, largely because Fred promptly admitted to having done that, the investigation never expanded to other students and other staff looking for other similar events. In retrospect, Fred's activities three years later suggest that a thorough investigation in the first instance would have developed inappropriate sexually gratifying contact with other female students in addition to Amy. If that sort of investigation had been done and had, in fact, shown more than the one isolated event, Fred might have been dismissed earlier, meaning that those girls offended later, including Jan, would not have suffered any damage. His prompt admissions should not have been allowed to abort that process. Quite the opposite, Fred's admissions should have been viewed as the basis for additional concern.

This scenario is a good sketch of what a lawyer considering a civil claim against the school district or Fred or administrators or board members will be looking for; that earlier "opportunity" to act decisively, thus avoiding altogether the later injury. Because this is the accepted approach to civil damage claims, the traditional "head in the sand" mentality preferred by educators no longer makes any sense. Always attempt to learn whatever can be learned or, if you prefer, consider how foolish you will look when some investigator uncovers, years later, significant factual evidence which was there to be seen if you had only chosen to look a little further.

During the three-some years following the first investigation and decision to leave Fred in student contact, Fred was not cured. He should have been a continuing focus of concern. Once a teacher exhibits tendencies toward inappropriate behavior, there is no good reason to believe that he or she is going to completely give up those tendencies. That is true regardless of whether the teacher is required to undergo counseling or not. Here, Fred having gone through the counseling actually misled the administrators into believing he was cured. Fred should have been watched closely rather than being treated as rehabilitated.

Note that at the time of the second investigation, there was good cause to believe that Fred was engaging in inappropriate touching and perhaps sexual interaction with several students. Then, the traditional barrier between Fred's work life and his home life was breached by the contact with the estranged spouse. That worked out well in the sense that the information provided by the spouse justified the decision to look at the home life. But, what if she had refused to submit to interview or denied there was a problem? That does occur, especially when there are children involved and a need to maintain the teacher's income as a source of economic support for the children. However, when the decision is made to look at the home life, the "look" should be thorough and it ought not be considered satisfied by the comments or lack of comments from a spouse, even a disaffected spouse. A thorough look means going back several years. If that had been done here, it is likely that it would have proved there was information to be had three years earlier—meaning that the first investigation had not been done well. When necessary to prove a dismissal case, however, the fact that revisiting an earlier point in time may be embarrassing to school officials or even open the school district to liability is, generally, not a good reason not to look. Always attempt to learn what there is to be learned. If you can find it, you cannot hide it. A competent investigator will come along later and find it again and, also, find your attempted coverup.

Case 6: Joe, the Girl's Basketball Coach and Up to Sixty Former Female Students

Joe is now fifty-one years of age; he is a former high school teacher, a former girl's basketball coach, and former women's physical education teacher. He has a young son by his current wife, who is the second former student he has married. Following his plea of guilty to a molestation charge, he was imprisoned for life.

Fourteen years prior to Joe's undoing, Terri had moved with her small children to the small town of Pahrump, Nevada. She enrolled in an aerobics class, and shortly thereafter, the instructor, who was then married to Joe, announced she was leaving town. Terri asked why and found out the instructor had come home unexpectedly and found Joe in bed with a high school girl, a girl, incidentally, whom Joe later married. But Terri considered this conduct unconscionable for anyone, especially a teacher, and went to the school administration asking what was going to be done about it. The administrator she spoke to indicated that, without a complaining victim, nothing would be done. The "victim" was the high school girl who by then had become Joe's fiancée, and she was not complaining. Terri was not satisfied and began a personal quest to find other victims—persons who would come forward.

Terri was successful. She found victims who claimed to have been abused during the period from 1977 to 1994. By the time her quest had ended, Joe had been divorced from the girl he had been in bed with when the aerobics instructor/wife returned home and he had married his current wife, also a former student, who had since borne their first child, a son. As a result of Terri's efforts, a woman who was a former student came forward and complained to law enforcement officials. She reported that Joe had sexual relations with her repeatedly, at school, during a two-year period which ended when she was eighteen. The prosecution alleged that while the sexual intercourse was technically "voluntary" it was actually non-consensual because the girl's will had been overcome by a combination of threats, gifts, and showers of attention. In particular, this victim claimed Joe had threatened to lower her grades if she did not submit; that he bought her clothes and jewelry, allowed her to use his vehicle, provided money for repairs for her vehicle, and allowed her special privileges at school. There was circumstantial evidence supporting the girl's claims. For example, Joe kept a sleeping bag at school. The custodian had found used condoms in the trash from Joe's classroom. Other former students reported Joe had fondled them at school, one when she stayed after school to ask a question in the classroom. Another claimed to have been forcibly hugged and kissed in the women's locker room where Joe could be, since he was the girl's basketball coach and women's physical education teacher. Another victim reported having earlier complained to the administration that Joe was having sexual relations with her fifteen-year-old friend (who would not tell). This earlier student reportedly had been told (words to the effect), "It's your word against his." In order to shut this student up, she claimed to have been allowed to graduate a year early and, in fact, she had graduated early. Faced with all of this incriminating testimony, Joe pleaded guilty. Then, faced with all of the same incriminating evidence, the judge threw the book at Joe and sentenced him to life!

Psychological Analysis

Depending on how one views the TSAS syndrome, Joe represents either our least worrisome or our most worrisome case. We know that the most common coupling occurs between high school females and male teachers, yet these may be the least reported and we believe that many cases of this sort are never reported. As a society, at an age specified by law, we believe that juveniles have a right to choose their own sex partners and voluntarily engage in sexual intercourse. This age is usually specified as sixteen or eighteen. The "voluntary" sex partner may be a twenty-five-, thirty-five-, or even fifty-five-year-old teacher. The student is usually a female and is usually beyond the age of consent. Coercion may not even be an issue. Often, the typical female student has access to an automobile and the freedom to go where she chooses and stay out in the late evening hours. Our society tends to idolize young women and sees little wrong with older men wanting them. We make jokes about "dirty old men" or "lechers" but meanwhile, it is not illegal for a forty-year-old man to sexually desire an eighteen-year-old girl. But, from the school system's point of view, it is wrong. Increasingly, professional practice codes preclude even a consensual sexual relationship between a teacher and student in the same school district and many prohibit a consensual sexual relationship between a teacher and a partner who is a student in another school district in the same state. This is the case because, as a society, we recognize that it is bad educational policy to allow teachers to fornicate with students. Teachers are hired to instruct in academic and vocational subjects, not *hands-on* sex education.

We do not subscribe to the philosophy of an amoral society with everyone for himself or herself. We believe in a structured society where societal rules and roles are taught; where status differences in school are the basis for the teacher and administrator to impose discipline and the student to receive it. Propriety and boundaries within a school system are part of classroom learning. Our world is a tightly structured, role oriented society in which policemen, mail persons, bosses, airline pilots, and teachers agree to play specific roles. Some activities are carefully outlined in job descriptions and some are merely implied as a basis for trusted or familial interactions. Therefore, whereas incest upsets the normal expectations of family life, TSAS upsets the expectations of the school system.

Our world is a chaotic one, in which anyone can do anything to anyone. This is a world which we, as a society, find unacceptable. Judge Robert Bork's current bestseller, *Slouching towards Gomorrah*, highlights the declining morality of contemporary America. Joe is a good example of that decline. Joe sees students as sexual opportunities. Married or not, he seeks to teach sex education in a prone position. His use of rewards, threats, and grades, not to mention his status as a teacher, is clearly coercive. That is the case even if his victims are seventeen or eighteen and legally allowed to consent to sexual intercourse. When he was involved with a fifteen year old, he was clearly violating the law and was guilty of statutory rape. When this sort of person is allowed to continue his liaisons with students, he tarnishes the reputation of all teachers. He literally alters the moral atmosphere within the school and the community. While teachers may no longer stand beside priests and nuns and rabbis as personifications of virtue, there needs to be a modicum of respect for those in education. Joe's very existence takes away from that goal.

The standards of the school system are different than the standards of the church or the state. The standards of behavior applied to students, teachers, and administrators need to support public educational goals. Joe, by his bedding and fondling of his students, is subverting these goals. He is increasing the cynicism of what may be an ever increasingly corrupt world and his behavior should never be considered acceptable behavior. If colleagues and administrators allow Joe to continue as a TSAS then the task of teaching becomes more difficult for everyone. Neither he nor his colleagues should delude themselves into thinking that it is okay to leave a trail of used condoms and sleeping bags.

Legal Analysis

When Terri was able to locate earlier victims of sexual abuse, that fact alone made the school officials' failure to identify victims and stop the abuse legally inexcusable. Regardless of whether the person who eventually uncovers this sort of information is a disaffected patron or a highly trained investigator, disclosure of past events of this sort leaves the employing school district with no defense as to liability and, increasingly, may expose those earlier administrators who chose not to act to *personal* liability. I endorse that trend but feel it is too narrow; I believe that *all staff who knew or should have known* need to be exposed to personal liability. I include fellow teachers. The law needs to require that a reasonable suspicion must be reported or pursued. Here, any one of several facts could form the basis for that suspicion, including a sleeping bag at school, used condoms in the classroom trash, the complaint by the aerobics instructor, Joe being caught in bed with a female student, his later marrying that student, the earlier complaint by a female student about a sexual relationship between Joe and her fifteen-year-old girlfriend, or his marrying his present wife (a former student). Even an anonymous complaint can form that basis when there is other circumstantial evidence suggesting the anonymous complaint has merit. Here, at many points along the way, a thorough investigation would have developed other circumstances, which would have then corroborated the event, which formed the factual basis for beginning the investigation.

Joe should have been a "focus of concern" a long, long time ago. At the least, evidence and complaints suggested Joe had a problem. When that sort of person is kept around, he is everyone's problem too. He should not have been a girl's basketball coach or a women's physical education teacher or allowed in the girls' locker room.

The supposed judicial concepts that the teacher is innocent until proven guilty and that the victim must come forward and face the perpetrator are simply rationalizations for doing nothing. In the 1990s, administrators who embrace these concepts are punished for it. Hopefully, soon, any school employee, including fellow teachers, who embrace these concepts will be punished for it. Fellow teachers should not be immune from liability. The teacher is in a position of trust and has a familial relationship with students and that can be abused. Therefore, the persons in that relationship should not be trusted implicitly—instead, they need to be watched closely and continuously.

ADULT MALES AND MALE STUDENTS: THE MALE PEDOPHILE TEACHER

The overwhelming majority of teacher abuse cases involve a male teacher and student. Most of these involve a male teacher and a female student. But, a significant minority involve male students. The following are examples of teachers who engaged in chronic repetitive sexual abuse of male students.

Case 7: What about Harry ?

At the point in time when Harry and his wife made a full disclosure to Dr. Rubin, Harry was forty-five years of age and in a community sex offender treatment program. He was a mild appearing, somewhat effeminate sounding, bespectacled, intelligent man. Harry was married and had fathered two teenage children. Although he was inclined to minimize and deny, he did admit to abusing twenty-one victims in over 200 pedophiliac incidents.

With regard to his pedophilia, a profile of his victims showed that with the exception of one eighteen-year-old boy, his victims were all males between the ages of eleven and fourteen. Harry described his focus as follows.

"For a boy to fit my idea of mature, he would exhibit certain physiological features, such as boys go through when in puberty. They would be in that state of growing up but not yet achieving a lot of facial, chest, or pubic hair. A potential victim was normally in that changing voice stage. . . . For a boy to fit my idea of mature, he would have to meet additional physiological conditions such as, he would have to be cute in my estimation, he would have to have a normal build, not too fat nor too skinny, and he would have to be shorter than me. He would also have to have certain personality traits, such as friendly, yet not boisterous; conversational, yet not over talkative; naive, yet not totally ignorant; bright, yet not necessarily genius; and finally, he would have to indicate a trusting admiration for me.

"After I singled out a particular boy, I would begin the process of grooming. This process involved almost the same steps in every case.

"I would do a lot of things to gain the boy's confidence. I would explain things extremely carefully or take extra time with him or while explaining things, I would touch the boy in certain ways to indicate my liking for him, such as a pat or squeeze of his hand. These touching experiences would evolve with the relationship with the boy. In time, I would include hugging and even putting my face against his while leaning over his shoulder to observe his work. There were times when I would wink at him or give him special looks. All of these behaviors I would do as discreetly as possible, as not to arouse any suspicion on the part of the other students. But, looking back, I am sure the others notice much of my behavior, at least to some degree. Eventually, I would also place special treats on his desk before school began. This would occur after I had developed a relationship with the boy, so he would know where the treats came from. I would also write special coded notes to the boy. After many weeks or months of this type of grooming, I would move into phase two. At this point, I would begin to develop some type of a relationship with the boy's parents. I would groom them in many ways too. If we went to the same church, this was very easy. I would show an interest in helping them in any way that would permit me to become close to them. Soon, they would invite me to their home for dinner, or to go with their family on various outings, some of which were overnight. After gaining this confidence, I would invite the boy to go with me on various outings too; such as hiking, or skiing, or to a movie, or whatever. While involved in their experiences, I would do all within my ability to be a child on his level. I would become very physical with him, in that I would horse around with him, or just plain hold his hand, or even kiss the top of his head to show additional affection, yet nothing distinctly sexual. If for some reason, by accident or by design, we sat beside each other, I would place my foot and/or my leg against his, and I would often place my hand on his leg and squeeze it. I would do all I could to make him think of me as an equal to himself in terms of interests, except that I had a driver's license and a checkbook. . . . At this point I would introduce the subject of sex. I would tell off-colored jokes, or if I already knew the boy's interest in dirty jokes, I might tell even more explicit stories. The purpose of this was to draw the boy into feeling comfortable about telling his own set of jokes and dirty stories. . . . I would buy *Playboy* magazines . . . and let him examine them carefully. I would do everything I could to make sex sound like the most fun thing in the world, and that adults always did all they could to keep kids from finding out about this fun. After I was convinced that the boy was groomed sufficiently for some hands-on experience in sex, I would arrange for him to spend some time alone with me. . . . Now I would use one of these outings to talk the boy into allowing me to begin the sexual touching process. Again, I would couch all the behavior in the context of what it would be like to have a girl do this. . . ."

Harry was a teacher who had taught in several school districts. He got in trouble with a male student during his first teaching position. He then left teaching for a few years, during which time he worked as an air traffic controller. Then, he resumed teaching in a new position in another state. There, because of allegations that he had been involved with male students, he was asked to resign. During this time, his wife knew of his tendency to engage in homosexual pedophilia with his students. She tried, however, to believe his claims that he would not do this again. As a result, she stayed with him and bore him two children, a boy and a girl. After the children were born, Harry also ran a summer teen tour bus business and he took over a small, isolated church school in a small, rural community, where he was the teacher and administrator. This community was unaware of any previous sexual misbehaviors, and neither Harry nor his wife Mary informed them of this history. Several years later, Mary and the two children noticed Harry was integrating a young boy from the church into family activities. All suspected that he was engaging in inappropriate behavior with the boy. Harry vehemently and repeatedly denied he was doing so. Later, however, he admitted that he had, in fact, been engaging in homosexual pedophilia with this boy.

Psychological Analysis

There were earlier indicators present here. Harry had been abandoned by his mother and was then adopted by his aunt and uncle. Harry's wife described this aunt as a "perfectionistic, domineering pedophile." Apparently, Harry's aunt had been married four times and would never accept Mary. As a result, Mary believes that Harry engages in pedophilia as a way of getting back at this woman. Harry's father was a chronic alcoholic. On one occasion, Harry and some friends found Harry's father lying passed out in the street. Harry had expressed bitterness to Mary about his poor relationship with his father.

As a child, Harry had been overweight and other kids teased him about his weight. But, he had also gone on to be president of his class in every high school grade.

When Harry was five years old, he and his five-year-old niece had mutually explored each other's genitals. At age seven Harry was fondling other boys and also simulating intercourse with a girl of the same age. During his teenage years, Harry had sexual contact with both boys and girls. Harry later admitted enjoying pornography as a boy, but also feeling guilty about it because his family were church-goers. To his current age, Harry has continued his bisexual orientation.

Harry "loves" pubescent males. He is clearly fixated on this age group and cannot stay away from them. His twenty-five-year history of sexual involvement with young males demonstrates his powerful obsession and the great danger he poses to young people. In Harry's own words, we see the predator at work—his choice of victims, his slow and purposeful development of an increasingly intimate relationship, and finally, the physical and sexual conquest of his boyfriend.

His wife only now recognizes the severity of his problem but she knew of his homosexual pedophilia at the beginning of her marriage. Now the depth of his problem requires application of the most severe behavioral treatments that have been developed. Even then, he will remain a risk to the community. The teaching situation is especially wrong for Harry because it permits him to develop the love relationship that he needs. He seems unconcerned with the damage he is doing to students.

Legal Analysis

Historically, stories of this sort are common. Traditionally, the homosexual pedophile was found out, or at least suspected, and asking for his resignation quietly eased him out. The resignation was usually innocuous, saying he was leaving for personal reasons or wished to move to another district or some such reason. In order to get rid of him it was often important that he be employable. Therefore, more often than not, neither his evaluation nor his personnel file made any reference to the pedophilia. When a written or telephone reference check would later come in, the administrator handling the matter would often stand ready to respond affirmatively if someone asked the magic question, "Has he been a child molester?" But, if no one asked, that information would not be volunteered. In some cases, rationalizing that there was no more than a suspicion or an unconfirmed claim by a student or by a few students, the administrator would deny any incidents of pedophilia took place at all.

This is a sort of "twenty-one questions" mentality, which presumes the molester is innocent until literally proven guilty or must be given the benefit of the doubt; the receiving employer, who is contemplating putting this person in contact with children, has a *duty* to ask the magic question. This is nonsense. It is the sort of approach that society has become fed up with—the root cause of much of society's loss of faith in teachers and administrators. In order to deal with this mind-set—society has, so to speak, lowered the bar—various remedies are available. The receiving school district, where Harry abuses a future child for example, when sued by that newly abused child, can claim against the district that allowed Harry to leave without taking disciplinary action against him and without fully disclosing the reasons for Harry's dismissal to the new employer. Now, when future injury occurs, that earlier district can claim over against Harry and against his marital community, including Mary. In practice, this means that the burden of disclosure has shifted from the inquirer to the person being asked, meaning that the person (or entity) with necessary information has an affirmative duty to disclose, regardless of how the inquiry is framed.

Most states now have a statute, which requires every adult who knows of child abuse to report it to police or child protective services; these laws do not respect attorney–client privilege or health care–patient privilege or husband–wife privilege. Mary had a duty to report and she failed to do so. She violated the law.

Notice that Harry spent some time running a summer "teen tour bus" and he also was the teacher and administrator of a small church. When school officials know that a suspected pedophile is going to be put into contact with children whom he might abuse, even though that relationship is not "public employment" and even though it does not result in a "teacher–student relationship," there is a duty to report, a duty to forewarn for a foreseeable risk. Waiting for someone to make a specific inquiry or even waiting for someone to make a general inquiry about Harry does not fulfill this duty. The duty can only be fulfilled by the person who knows or who has a reasonable suspicion to be proactive by going to the class of persons who need to be warned and making a full and complete disclosure about Harry. The duty (or obligation) is owed to every child, not just those in public school or private schools. For example, when we have legitimate concerns about Harry and know Harry is there, the duty may flow to the students on the summer "teen tour bus" driven by Harry or to the students in the rural church where Harry is choir director. In my opinion, when an employee is let go for proven or suspected pedophilia, and he is later seen as a choir director or scout master or grid kid coach or chaperone or any other role involving occasional unsupervised contact with students, there is a duty to warn. Realize that when we warn, we expose ourselves to claims by Harry that we have invaded his privacy or injured his business reputation, but warn—always warn.

Unlike the card no one wants in the "Old Maid" card game, a teacher is not relieved of personal duty by passing the information to a principal. Passing the information to a superintendent does not relieve a principal. These duties are personal and they flow from the person who possesses the knowledge to the person who should be fully informed in order to protect children in that person's charge. A subordinate who informs a superior, hoping (or presuming) that superior will pass on the information, only exposes him or herself to greater liability, if the requisite warning does not issue to the person who needs to hear it.

A pedophile may exhibit evidence of pedophilia at work or in his private life. When evidence arises at work, the public employer can focus concern on the employee's private life but must do so carefully. In this case, the employer with suspicions needed to recheck the employee's work history and contact previous employers and supervisors. A suspicion about pedophilia with a current thirteen year old can be confirmed by reports of prior suspicions by prior employers or supervisors. Similarly, suspicion by a current co-worker or student can be confirmed by previous student sources. A pedophile usually will present a pattern, and, once there is suspicion that a pattern exists, investigation should narrow. Here, we know that Harry preferred boys aged eleven to fourteen and once that sort of suspicion arises, the suspicion ought to dictate the parameters of the search.

As a general rule, public school employers should search back for up to six years for patterns. Usually, a tendency to misbehave will become evident during that length of time. The six-year rule is not, however, a hard and fast rule. In one recent case, a current complaint led to review of a ten-year-old event which presented the same homosexual grooming pattern. In that case, the grooming took the form of presents for students' birthdays and holidays and trips to a Shakespearean festival in Oregon with consequent overnight stays in motels. The first time, the teacher was admonished, but nine years later, at age fifty-five, he repeated the same pattern.

Here, we see a classic example of progressive grooming techniques. Usually, even if the actual outcome of sexual abuse cannot be confirmed, other students will notice the grooming. The grooming itself had no educational purpose and can form the factual basis for "sufficient cause" to remove the teacher from further contact with students. Note here, the wife and children noticed the grooming with the boy he brought into the family activities.

In some cases, other students who observed this sort of thing will recall it as something that they found offensive, as something they feared in the sense that they feared the teacher would do it to them, too. In some cases, the student will not remember what he or she observed or overheard that was considered offensive, but they will have an opinion, e.g., "He was weird" or "I never wanted to be alone with him." When asked why, many sources will support the initial opinion with another opinion, e.g., "Because he was strange." Occasionally, repeated attempts to elicit a factual foundation for the opinion will be unsuccessful. But, in some cases the source will report bothersome events, e.g., "He would run his hands through kids' hair in a weird way."

Some of what is reported above as now known about Harry is, realistically, not going to be discovered by the current employer. Harry's wife knew but she had a vested interest in Harry maintaining his profession, his income, and the family unit. The wife willing to stay with a pedophile will usually cling to some belief that the pedophile will not reoffend. Similarly, Harry's children cannot be expected to report him; who wants to admit to him or herself that Dad is a pedophile?

When suspicions first arise, it is usually a bad idea to investigate the employee's home life or private life. The probable cause to investigate the employee's private life has to be factual and it has to be substantially or quantitatively close to that needed to dismiss. Therefore, as a general rule, the close look at the private life comes only after other factual suspicions arising at the workplace have been confirmed to the extent that a work life probable cause is provable. Then, further support may be found in the private life.

Private life sources include neighborhood checks with persons in the target age group (for Harry, eleven- to fourteen-year-old boys) who previously resided in the same neighborhood with the suspected employee; target group representatives who the suspect employee may have interacted with, for example, as a youth soccer coach or youth soccer or football referee or scout leader.

Point–Counterpoint

In general, there is none. Both the psychologist and the attorney believe that this is the most dangerous individual in the community and all involvement with children must be avoided.

Psychologist: We do have one potential disagreement. The home life, work life distinction is especially important to me. I would take the position that private home activity or private sexual behavior is off-limits to school personnel unless there is a demonstrated relationship between private behavior and risk to students. Many individuals who engage in sexually aberrant behavior privately will never engage in dangerous or illegal behavior at school. It would be an invasion of privacy to force them to disclose their private behaviors or fantasies. This is done in treatment of sex offenders because (a) they have committed a sexual crime and (b) we believe their thinking and fantasies relate to the probability of future crimes. We demand that they disclose . . . but we often do not trust them. We demand polygraph examinations and wife participation as further evidence of their private sexuality.

Attorney: Anything is apparently possible. We agree. Note that Dr. Rubin will allow the look at private life only if there is a "demonstrated relationship" and that is exactly what society requires. Basically, if school officials are going to look into a teacher's private life, they had better have a provable reason to do it or they will be sued individually and may not own their own house the following year. This is as it should be. The administrator does not get to judge what is a "demonstrated relationship." That is a legal test and it should only be applied after a detailed consult with the school attorney, who had also better be right if he or she wishes to continue to represent that school district!

Case 8: Then There Was Charlie!

Charlie was a music teacher who offended as he was about

to begin his third year with Desert District in the state of Washington. He was about forty years old, he was married, and he had a nine-year-old daughter. Charlie and his wife were active in a local church, where Charlie was the choir director. His wife's father was a minister and both Charlie and his wife had previously been active in churches in other communities. This was Charlie's first marriage and he had been married for about sixteen years. His wife had been his high school sweetheart.

According to information in his personnel file, Charlie had last worked as a teacher in the state of Idaho about ten years prior, where he worked in one district for one year and then moved to a second district for an additional two years. He then had a break in teaching during which time he worked in private industry in southern California. He returned to teaching, working for one year at Cedar, a western Washington school district and then transferred to Desert District. When he began his employment at Cedar, he had filled out the usual pre-employment questionnaire, which asked if he had ever been arrested or convicted of any crime other than minor traffic violations. Charlie replied "no." When he moved to Desert, he filled out much the same questionnaire and again reported "no" to any prior arrests or convictions.

In the 1980s, when Charlie began his employment in the state of Washington, that state vetted (investigated) new teachers by conducting a criminal record data screen of *Washington State records only*. This was done by the Washington State Patrol and resulted in a negative report—Charlie had no arrests or convictions in Washington.

Both at Cedar schools and again at Desert schools, Charlie was hired to teach elementary and middle school music. He had excellent academic qualifications and it was soon apparent that Charlie was an excellent music teacher with good instructional skills and good interpersonal teacher-to-student relationship skills. Kids and their parents liked Charlie. But, there were fundamental problems with Charlie. He was a pedophile and he was a liar.

Charlie had been arrested before and convicted before. He had been arrested for disorderly conduct and prostitution in

California. He had also been arrested in California for indecent exposure and disorderly conduct. These charges related to homosexual sexual contacts in public parks. Charlie had submitted to a program of sex therapy counseling. He had successfully completed that program in the sense that he had attended all the sessions. As a result, California had let him change his plea to "not guilty" on charges already brought and told him that as far as California was concerned, he had never been arrested or convicted of anything. This means his record was "expunged." Charlie had engaged in some homosexual contacts in Idaho, too. Those had led to his being asked by his first school district to leave and further contacts had led to his second school employer issuing a notice of dismissal. For those reasons, he had gone to California.

One day in the late summer of 1990, Charlie was at the local municipal pool for a swim with his nine-year-old daughter. While there, his attention was attracted by a teenage boy. Charlie couldn't help but overhear this boy's conversation with his friends and it was soon apparent to Charlie that Ed was a resident at a local juvenile group home. This was a minimum security home which focused primarily on education of its residents, preparing them for parole to their home community. That day at the pool, Ed was seventeen years old and felt he was going on twenty-five. He loved to brag about his past. While Charlie listened, he told his fellows how he had intercourse with his own sister when he was nine and how he had run away from home; he claimed to have fathered children in several communities, and was in the group home for raping a teenage girl. He also bragged about having had homosexual relationships with truck drivers in return for rides around the West Coast. This last claim rang some old bells with Charlie. Even though he had fathered a child, he was a homosexual and he began to look at Ed with increased interest.

Charlie engaged Ed in conversation and heard a new twist to the rape story. According to Ed, he had consensual intercourse rather than rape and since he had watched the intercourse his stepdad could clear him, except that he was an illegal alien and, if he came forward, he would be deported. So Ed had to take the rap for the rape. He indicated that he was not adverse to doing time for the rape because he was wanted in

Utah for pushing a boy off the second floor of a building and besides, Ed wanted to settle down and learn to be a potter or a counselor or a lawyer and maybe a part-time musician. Charlie could not resist all of this nonsense; he began planning how he could get Ed over to his house and molest him. Charlie then called the group home and arranged to have Ed mow his lawn. After the mowing, Charlie proposed a soda and offered to show Ed his collection of musical instruments. He took Ed to the basement where they spent a while examining the musical instruments.

Then Charlie suggested that Ed allow him to take Polaroid pictures of Ed's penis. Ed found that interesting and managed to get an erection. Charlie took several pictures of it. Charlie began to propose several forms of sexual intercourse. Ed claimed that he asked if someone else would be around and Charlie said no, he'd arranged for his wife and daughter to be away. By the time the day was over, Charlie and Ed both had oral and anal intercourse with each other.

Ed promptly returned to the group home and reported the entire matter to the group home supervisor. The supervisor called the police. The police promptly procured a search warrant, went to Charlie's house, and found the Polaroid pictures and towels containing pubic hairs, fecal material, and lubricants. When the police arrived with the warrant, both Charlie and his wife Vera, who indicated that this was not the first time Charlie had done this, met them. Charlie had no defense and confessed to the whole incident. Ed's version of events was confirmed.

When the police interviewed Ed, he indicated that he had submitted to the intercourse with Charlie because he believed Charlie would hurt him if he did not submit. When he was younger and living in another state, there had been a molester in the area who had taken photographs of victims, then had sexual relations with them, and then killed them. But, one wonders. Ed was not a particularly credible source. His true motivation for reporting was never entirely clear, but was probably related to Charlie having only paid him $10, Ed having made a passing comment that Charlie got more than $10 worth of services.

Charlie was suspended from teaching and shortly issued a

notice of dismissal. The dismissal process took several months, during which Charlie continued to be paid pursuant to his teaching contract. Eventually, however, Charlie could delay no further on the criminal charges against him. He pleaded guilty to having sexually assaulted Ed, thus ending his salary payments and his teaching career.

Charlie's wife and daughter left him. He was sentenced to the county jail but much of the sentence was suspended. It seemed to the school district that the matter was over. But not so. The education association insisted on taking the matter to arbitration. It contended that Charlie had not abused any students in his employing district, and as the tryst with Ed had occurred during the summer months, he had not abused anyone during the school year. Therefore, the association argued, he should be reinstated to his teaching position.

The education association suggested that Charlie might benefit from a leave of absence during which time he would work on sex therapy and rehabilitation. The association also suggested that in order to assist Charlie in his rehabilitation, he should be paid during his leave of absence, insisting that continued salary payments be a condition to any such settlement. Finally, the association, perhaps tongue-in-cheek, insisted that Charlie should also be guaranteed a teaching contract for the next teaching year. The school district found the education association's position to be incredible and responded by preparing a declaratory judgment action, which is a form of lawsuit. Faced with the prospect of this lawsuit being filed and public disclosure of its position being made in the local news media, the education association reconsidered and Charlie finally resigned. Later, the Washington State Superintendent of Public Instruction took Charlie's teaching certificate and it is unlikely that Charlie will ever teach again.

Psychological Analysis

Charlie's case makes us realize that the backgrounds of many teacher-offenders are squeaky clean. A good marriage, church involvement, no criminal record, all of which would make anyone think that this forty year old is all right. Actually, closer investigation did find previous sex crimes and immoral involvements. We all still harbor stereotypes that sex offenders should have a horrible history of multiple victims and that only wild, out of control young people commit sexual offenses against children. Sorry, it isn't so!

Charlie engaged in what was substantially a voluntary sexual relationship with Ed. There was no mention of force and there were no threats. Ed's motivations are unclear. It is possible that Ed actually trapped Charlie and did it to get back at his father or previous authority figures. Freud used the term "transference" to label the feeling a patient has for his/her doctor and "counter transference" for the feeling a doctor has for his/her patient. It attempts to reveal why we carry over feelings from a previous relationship into a new, present relationship. One of the least understood aspects of human behavior is their passion for the object, which may symbolize or signify something else. Crosses, religious icons, works of art, all may have meaning far from the obvious and this may also include sexual behavior.

The flaws in the system of background checks evidenced by Charlie's story show that we are not getting full knowledge of the histories of teacher applicants. Charlie's wife knew of his pedophilic tendencies and perhaps should either have pushed Charlie to get treatment or insisted that he never teach again. At what point should the spouse intervene? Is Charlie a threat to his students? Many individuals within the confines of the classroom control their impulses and fantasies. There is no evidence that Charlie had engaged in sexual behavior with students. Still, the possibility exists. Further, his reputation in the community will influence how students, parents, and peers respond to Charlie in the future.

Legal Analysis

Note that following the beginning of the investigative suspension, as long as the matter was treated in confidence, as most personnel matters are, it was going nowhere. Charlie was getting paid while he was on suspension. He had no motivation to bring either the relationship with his employing school district or the criminal charges pending against him to closure. His motivation was to delay and delay.

The education association probably had no use for Charlie and felt no better about him than management. But, the education association worried about "fair representation" claims wherein a teacher such as Charlie could claim that more could have been done and that he was treated adversely as a result of poor representation. Fearing these claims, education associations will often take positions that make no sense to anyone, including those taking the position.

Notice that potential publicity in the form of a lawsuit finally brought this matter to closure. But, a school district cannot summarily choose to make a matter of this sort public. Doing that is going to expose the entire matter and given what Charlie had done here, the public does not really care whether a hearing officer or arbitrator finds for the district or Charlie; very simply, the public will not tolerate someone like Charlie coming back into teaching. They do not care about sex therapy or promises or assurances. Letting the public know Charlie exists is akin to deciding never to let Charlie back. Therefore, it is essential to be right, because if information of this sort is exposed to public scrutiny and it is erroneous, and Charlie is really not the sexual predator he appears to be, Charlie is going to have a very significant civil action for loss of business reputation. Publicity is a two-edged sword and to keep faith with union bargaining representatives and attorneys and our internal dispute resolution processes, it is usually best to avoid it. Incidentally, that could have been done here; no arbitrator was going to put Charlie back to work and, consequently, if the school district had entered into arbitration, the downside was paying Charlie for several more months while the arbitration was pending. Nothing more.

The education association's proposal that Charlie get a leave of absence and undergo sex offender treatment during this absence while getting paid was a laughable proposal—and the education association knew it. No one on that side of the table expected that offer to be accepted by management. The offer was made to avoid a "fair representation" claim by Charlie.

Point–Counterpoint

Psychologist: The penalties imposed were light but I believe they were fair. My co-author is obviously perturbed that the district is paying, but at some point I believe that the school system and the teacher's union should pay for therapy. The problem, I believe, is one of the occupational hazards of teaching.

Generally, the problem of sexual involvement with students can be effectively treated and especially should be treated if teachers and their colleagues become aware of these tendencies. In the ideal system, the teacher would acknowledge this tendency and seek treatment while still employed. Situational safeguards would be put in place such as never being alone with students, after school or on trips. The teacher as a valued professional would be cared for and maintained on the job. If Charlie is ever to teach again, then perhaps the district and the union need to shoulder some of the treatment costs. However, if he will not be allowed to return to teaching then I, too, would be distressed if he continues to receive financial support in the form of continued wages.

I add a general comment: Charlie had prior sex therapy and obviously, he reoffended. Persons like Charlie need to be controlled or changed rather than cured. He is responsible for his actions and not merely the victim of an illness. We actually have great success with sex offender treatment programs. Many of these programs are successful in helping the perpetrator to keep his behavior under his own control, as opposed to curing him.

Attorney: Charlie should not be allowed to return to teaching. Dr. Rubin's logic is not only flawed, it is wasting taxpayer dollars and putting future students at risk. Charlie's "employment rights" arise from a collective bargaining agreement the students and parents never agreed too. To regain the confidence of the public, teachers like Charlie have to go and then stay gone.

The boy he molested here is generally of student age. It will not be difficult for Charlie to find other boys with generally similar backgrounds within the school system. I see Charlie as a proven danger to students. Still, Dr. Rubin's comments do raise a legitimate societal concern. Whether he is teaching or not, Charlie continues to pose a danger to society and he ought to be in treatment. I am bothered by the school district and perhaps teacher's union paying for that treatment because I am confident that neither the school system nor union wanted persons like Charlie in the system in the first place. But he did manage to get into the system. Now what? Should society essentially punish the school system and union by forcing them to pay fair shares to rehabilitate Charlie? Perhaps, but at least we should admit that is being done.

Case 9: Orville Allen Longuskie, a Homosexual Pedophile

Orville Longuskie began teaching in 1968 on the island of Guam. Before his first year of teaching had concluded, he had been arrested and charged with lewd conduct with a male student who claimed Longuskie had molested him. The eleven-year-old boy claimed that Longuskie had taken his clothes off, kissed him, taken nude pictures of him, and sexually molested him. There was a jury trial and Longuskie was acquitted. Guam officials then paid off his contract and terminated his service.

Longuskie then came to the state of Washington where he served relatively brief stints in various small school districts. In 1969–70 he taught in Quincy, then Hartline, then Burbank, then Pateros, then he went to California for three years, returning to Taholah, and finally going to Kahlotus. Each of the Washington districts was quite small, with no more than a few hundred total students, grades K–12. At Kahlotus, for example, there was a total, altogether, of twelve administrators and teachers.

At Taholah, a small district with teacher cottages, staff noted that Longuskie had papered over the windows of his cabin with black paper. Later, at Pateros, where he taught at the fifth- and sixth-grade level, there had been a sheriff's investigation. Longuskie had been taking boys on trips and staying overnight in motels with them. The boys were about twelve years of age and there were several. One was ten years old and Longuskie took him to a motel on three occasions. Boys reported that Longuskie liked to rub their feet, their legs, and would offer them beer and champagne. He also would undress in front of the boys. The Sheriff's Office recommended an arrest warrant be issued, but no evidence could later be found showing the sheriff's investigation was ever reported to the school. However, for whatever reason, Longuskie was allowed to leave the school district and there was no follow-up by law enforcement or prosecution. Later, when applying at Kahlotus (see below) he reported that at Pateros he "was again commended for . . . teaching and classroom control." He then went to California where he began employment as a security guard.

Later, at Burbank, Longuskie took male students on trips to Hawaii. One boy lived with Longuskie for several years, and when Longuskie left Burbank for Pateros, the boy went with him. Longuskie eventually became this boy's legal guardian. Later, after events unfolded at Kahlotus, a student was found who reported seeing Longuskie and this male student in bed together. Although he failed to mention these facts, when he applied at Kahlotus (see below), he did report that "upon leaving [Burbank] I received an award of commendation for outstanding contribution to the community."

At Kahlotus, when he arrived at the beginning of the 1986–87 school year, Longuskie was forty-seven years old. He had never married and had no children. In 1967, he had graduated from Central Washington State College with a major in education and minor in music. Since his graduation he had finished an additional forty-one quarter hours, focusing especially on music and opera. Throughout this period, Longuski had been a student of the opera and he claimed to be an accomplished opera singer who had sung in operas throughout North America and in Europe.

At Kahlotus, he befriended a sixth-grade boy. This boy came from a dysfunctional, single-parent family. Longuskie, on the other hand, was viewed as an excellent teacher and his focus on the boy did, in fact, result in dramatic improvement in the boy's school grades. The boy was overweight and school staff all reported him to be a marginal achiever. During his time with Longuskie, he lost weight and began to interact in class. But, there was bizarre behavior that accompanied this change.

Longuskie and the boy would ask others in the town to hide them from the boy's father. They would literally hide for hours at a time in vehicle garages. The boy would sometimes spend days at a time living with Longuskie, but those who had seen Longuskie's cabin noted there was only one bed in it. Longuskie would send the boy notes at school, using other students to courier these notes back and forth. Longuskie did not want the boy around other students; he would insist on watching the boy when the boy was swimming or interacting with others. Also, Longuskie admonished the boy to avoid female students, even the boy's own sister. Longuskie insisted that the boy sign the following list of "promises":

"I will stay with Mr. Longuskie until I am married. I will not touch girls in any way, including my sister. I will not go to my sister's bedroom. I will sleep as usual (always) including affection. I will not go to [girl's] volleyball games this year. I will not *ever* tell Mr. Longuskie 'I do not want to stay with you'. . . ."

For a while, Longuskie was paying the boy's father $30 a week, apparently to continue the association on an amicable basis. He also spent lavishly on the boy, so lavishly that, by October 1988, he was bankrupt with $44,400 in debts accumulated from twelve separate credit cards.

In January 1989, ironically while Longuskie was in the process of attempting to get legal guardianship allowing him to assume a court-approved parenting role with the boy, Longuskie's activities caught up with him. A complaint was received, saying in part, "as parents of students . . . under direct supervision of this teacher . . . we feel that his obsession with a student is beyond the role of teacher." Then, Longuskie's world began to unravel. At about this time, community members using the public school gym one evening overheard Longuskie yelling at the boy, in the boys' locker room with the lights out. A school board meeting was scheduled to deal with the parent complaint referred to above, and apparently believing he was going to lose the boy, Longuskie kidnapped the boy and the two began to hide out in a motel some fifty miles from Kahlotus. Then, Longuskie appeared at the school board meeting concerning the complaint but denied knowledge of the boy's whereabouts (the boy was then waiting for Longuskie in the motel room). However, by now the Sheriff's Office was involved and, at one point, there was a forty-five-mile car chase with the Sheriff's Office in pursuit, and a local rancher keeping track of Longuskie with a private plane. The boy was found, temporarily placed in a foster home, and Longuskie was arrested, yet he was not done. He was released on his own recognizance with the admonition that he not contact the boy. Within forty-eight hours, he was attempting to determine the boy's location. He then attempted to get to the boy through a friend, offering the boy a 4×4 if the boy would run away with him.

Later, search warrants were utilized to examine Longuskie's cabin and his vehicle. It became apparent that Longuskie had collected photographs of the boy in Kahlotus and other boys, some of whom were never fully identified. He was also collecting pubic hair from the towels in the boy's locker room.

The superintendent issued Longuskie a notice of dismissal and the teacher's association appealed the dismissal. Longuskie was then charged with kidnapping in the first degree and attempted kidnapping in the first degree. His bail was raised from $10,000 to $100,000. The school district then took the position that since he could not get out of jail to teach, the district had no duty to pay him. Longuskie, by the education association, responded by threatening to sue for back wages and attorney fees. Next, Longuskie attempted to hire his soon to be released cellmate to get the boy's father. Then, some five months after his arrest, Longuskie was found guilty. The teacher's association finally withdrew support and the state superintendent of public instruction took Longuskie's teaching certificate. Although he had initially denied sexual contact, at Longuskie's trial the boy testified to repeated acts of oral and anal sodomy. Also at this trial, two of the boys he had molested in Pateros ten years earlier testified against him. The trial judge, at sentencing, noted that Longuskie had "selected the Kahlotus boy as a victim because he was vulnerable, had a low intellect, and family problems . . . [and that] after gaining the boy's trust, he had molested [him]."

Psychological Analysis

It is clear that Mr. Longuskie has a lifelong sexual problem. It would have been better if, after his initial problem in Guam, a permanent record followed him. If he truly was acquitted, then why was his contract terminated? Even if he was not "not guilty" of a crime he should have been removed from teaching. The standard, which we apply to teaching, is not and need not be the same as applied in a criminal proceeding.

This teacher moved a great deal and that alone should make an administrator a bit wary. His odd behavior, such as papering over his windows, does not mean that he is a sex offender, but behavior of this sort ought to raise general suspicions. Clearly, overall review makes it clear that inadequate communication between school employers and law enforcement agencies allowed Mr. Longuskie to continue his teaching career and consequent molestation of young men.

Mr. Longuskie presents as a lonely man without the peer relationships that are evidence of a healthy psychological status. He seemed to gravitate to or choose unhappy lads to befriend. He probably told himself that he was doing it for their own good. Note that his "devotion" to his students was considered remarkable and even won him commendations. But, his interest in the chosen "boy" went far beyond educational concerns. He was watchful, jealous, and controlling. Much like a jealous lover, he wants sole rights to his student. Other staff must have noticed this. Colleagues should be watching out for *all* students and should be watching all colleagues. In my opinion, in this small teaching community, someone should have noticed the obsessive behavior and challenged it much sooner.

Mr. Longuskie's problems go beyond some minimal sexual activity. He is a very disturbed man who seeks to own his chosen student. He selects vulnerable children and sadly, furthers their own psychological destruction. He needs their love and is scared of losing it. His sexual obsessions seem to dominate his life and one wonders how no one supposedly noticed his actions.

Almost without exception, the teacher's association or union needs to defend its members. However, Mr. Longuskie's history and problems are difficult to defend and perhaps Mr. Longuskie is a good example of a person who should not be defended. Instead, perhaps the teacher's organization needs to more carefully evaluate its members on an ongoing basis.

Legal Analysis

I have always found this case especially annoying. Longuskie should have been stopped at least ten years earlier than he was. For whatever reason, the Pateros situation ended badly and probably contributed to abuse of children in Burbank, Kahlotus, and perhaps at other locations. Because of situations of this sort, case law has now turned against administrators who fail to act properly in abating one of these situations and, as a result, personal liability can now attach. In the situation at bar, assume that the boy in Kahlotus and his parents sued Kahlotus School District; that district would then sue other districts that it claimed needed to have acted earlier, including, for example, Pateros, which might sue the former administrators, claiming they acted outside the scope of employment by failing to terminate Longuskie and failing to report him to the professional practices division, state superintendent of public instruction.

In 1990, a year after Longuskie was apprehended, the state of Washington enacted a rule requiring that a school superintendent who "possesses sufficient reliable information to believe" that a teacher or other certificated employee is "not of good moral character or personally fit or has committed an act of unprofessional conduct" must report that to the state and if that is not done, the state can move against the certificate of the superintendent who should have reported and did not. Also, in 1990, the state of Washington enacted a code of professional conduct applicable to teachers and other certificated employees. Since Longuskie, all persons applying for a Washington teaching certificate must submit to a fingerprint criminal identification check; that would have disclosed the 1968 Guam action if it had been done earlier when Longuskie came to Washington and began teaching in 1969.

The education association defended Longuskie, claiming he was eccentric and nothing more. Attempts to learn his true history in Guam were resisted by the association, as was the attempt to terminate him and the attempt to terminate his salary. The association had to do this in order to protect itself against a "fair representation" claim by Longuskie that surely would have followed if it (the association) had chosen not to represent him. But, "fair representation" aside, this man was not entitled to a defense, he was a predator and then became a predator incarcerated in a county jail with a $100,000 bail and even then, the association continued to represent him. The point at which the association cuts these sorts of persons loose and refuses further representation needs to come earlier in the process than it does now.

Note that some of the eventual evidence against Longuskie came from his lifestyle and his private life. The Longuskie case is an example of how our insistence on a clear distinction between the teacher's work life and home life can make it more difficult than it ought to be to weed out a predator.

Finally, Longuskie became a *state-level* problem who eventually taught and perhaps abused in six separate local school districts. But the state did nothing at all until after Longuskie was dismissed at Kahlotus. Throughout, the state treated him as a *local-district*–level problem. Notice, though, that Longuskie always opted for the smaller districts, the ones that lacked a human resources director or personnel director. That was not a coincidence. Smaller school districts need to be supported by a personnel department at a mid-state level, which will allow them to make hiring decisions and investigative decisions as competently as those made by large urban districts.

Case 10: An Obsessive Homosexual Pedophile— Elementary PE Specialist

Phil was a physical education specialist, which is a classification of teacher used at the elementary level to provide physical education training to both boys and girls, usually in mixed classes. A mid-year PE specialist vacancy had unexpectedly occurred at a K–5 elementary school and Phil applied. He had most recently worked for a neighboring district, which we'll call the Kinder District. He had served Kinder as a PE specialist at the elementary level for most of a school year, in a position as "long-term substitute" (meaning more than a month and less than an entire school year). That was exactly the sort of situation he applied for at the district in question, which we'll call the Pride District.

Phil was about forty years of age, well groomed, well dressed, and personable. He interviewed well and within a few days of beginning his duties, both his new principal and teachers in the building reported that he fit in well with existing faculty. Phil came to Pride District with a strong letter of recommendation from the principal of the elementary building he had served in Kinder District. His evaluation from Kinder District was equally impressive. Beyond that, little was known about Phil. He was single, lived alone, had no social acquaintances among teaching staff in the area, and had moved to the state about a year earlier. He applied for and, based upon certification in another state, was issued a state teaching certificate, and had been endorsed in elementary PE.

Shortly after Phil began his duties, he began asking fifth-grade boys to go on private field trips with him. He had a dog and he would ask them to go with him while he walked the dog by the river. Then, as ski season began, he started asking fourth- and fifth-grade boys if they would like to go skiing with him. One of these boys asked his mom if he could go and she told the dad, who called the principal to determine all the specifics about what he assumed was a school activity. This was the principal's first notice that Phil was issuing these personal invitations. Since the trip was neither a school activity nor even approved, the principal called Phil in to discuss these extracurricular activities and why Phil was not to be interacting with the students outside of the school day unless he was involved in an approved school activity. Phil agreed but, as spring approached, there were rumors that Phil was talking to the fifth-grade boys about plans for a camping trip over spring vacation; specifically, a canoeing trip into Canada.

About that time, the fifth-grade class was going on its annual field trip to a large city. This was a trip that Mary, the fifth-grade teacher had been planning with her class all year long. The trip was to be held over spring break and Mary needed another chaperone. Phil volunteered and was accepted. He then accompanied the fifth-grade class to Seattle. In the van on the way, Mary noted that Phil enjoyed "horsing around" with the boys, sort of tickling and wrestling with them, and she had to counsel him not to do that. On this trip, all the boys slept in one room of a church and the girls in another. Part of Phil's job was to monitor the sleeping area and get the boys up in the morning. Phil performed his wake-up task by getting on the floor, with the boys in sleeping bags, and rolling around on the floor, tickling and wrestling with them to get them up. This was reported to Mary and she began to be concerned.

Mary was not concerned enough to remove Phil, but she was concerned enough to begin "focusing" her attention and advising parents on the trip, in a guarded way, to do the same. When the class returned to Pride, the kids were asked to prepare a report on their trip, including a drawing. One boy drew a ferryboat and put a note on it, "[Phil] is a ferry," with a picture of Phil waving from the ferryboat. That was enough for Mary. She then went to the principal and expressed concern about Phil. She noted that she had "done some checking" and found that the girls felt Phil didn't even like them, that he ignored them during PE and always called on the boys and spent his time with the boys. The principal then reported this new concern to the personnel director, who then contacted the personnel director in Kinder District, asking if there had been any problems of that sort there. The personnel director in Kinder District did not report any problems, but he seemed, to the personnel director in Pride District, to be uncomfortable talking about Phil. The personnel director in Pride decided to check further. He called the personnel director in another adjoining district, primarily to see if there had been any problems with Phil when he had substituted in that district. He knew this other personnel director lived in Pride District and had a boy attending the school Phil was assigned to. This personnel director reported that he had experienced no work-related problems with Phil, but he had cause to wonder when Phil had recently asked his son to go on a weekend hike. The Pride personnel director then determined that Phil had solicited the boy several weeks after his principal had admonished him not to do that sort of thing. Concern now heightened.

Informal checks were begun with local law enforcement officials in the Kinder District where Phil lived. The inquiry focused on whether there had been any problems of any sort with Phil. The checks revealed that Phil had been the subject of a police investigation in Kinder about a year earlier, when a mother had reported that Phil had taken her fourth-grade boy snow sledding. Phil had been the boy's teacher at Kinder and had invited the boy to sled with him after school. The mom had approved this and the two had gone off sledding on a local hill. They had both become soaking wet, and Phil had then suggested they go back to his apartment and dry off. At the apartment, in order to speed up the clothes drying, Phil had suggested that they strip and watch TV for awhile in the nude while their clothes dried. Then, according to the boy, he had fondled the boy's genitals. They had dressed and he had taken the boy home. When the boy reported the gist of this to his mom, she reported it to the police in Kinder, who began an investigation. But the investigation stopped when the school officials in Kinder said they would take care of it. They had counseled Phil and gave assurances to the boy's mother that Phil would not be inviting children out again because he would soon be leaving Kinder's service and probably leaving the area. The mom accepted these assurances from the school officials "on condition that Phil never teach again" and Kinder school officials had agreed. The mother then withdrew the complaint to the police. All of this information was relayed to the personnel director of Pride District who was incensed. He called his counterpart at Kinder, challenging him to explain what was going on. After all, the principal at Kinder had recommended Phil.

The principal, whom we will call Harriet, did not wish to talk about Phil. She would only say that she had received a complaint from a boy's mother about a sledding incident, which she reported to the personnel director. The teacher's association had become involved, and a representative of the association had suggested that, unless she could prove these allegations, she would find herself in a legal predicament. She agreed that this was good advice at the time and still thought so. She indicated that the mom had made no "formal complaint" against Phil; the mom had not made "a written statement." The boy's claims that he and Phil had been nude and that Phil had fondled him "couldn't be proven," and the matter had been turned over to the police. She had no idea where Phil was or what he was doing and she didn't want to know. Finally, she reported to the Pride personnel director that she had nothing further to say on the subject.

The personnel director shared with Harriet where Phil was teaching and what he was allegedly doing and that Phil probably wouldn't be there except for her glowing recommendation. Harriet responded that she was a professional, not used to being questioned this way and she was offended. Harriet was indignant as she slammed the phone down, thus ending the interview.

That left the Kinder Police Department. The Pride personnel director next contacted the police asking for a copy of their report on the investigation of the sledding incident. The police reported that without a release signed by Phil (as the suspect) or the boy and mother (as victim) they could not confirm or deny there was a report. Because of this roadblock, the personnel director of Pride made a formal written request to Phil to sign a release allowing the personnel director access to this file at the Kinder Police Department. Phil, now accompanied by his teacher's association representative, refused and indicated that if the personnel director persisted in attempting to get this information that it would violate Phil's privacy rights and he would sue the Pride District for injury to his professional reputation.

The Pride personnel director felt that all avenues were closed. The police department would not release the report without consent from Phil, who would not give it, or from the parent of the boy, who was as yet unidentified. Phil was working for Pride, and was in student contact on a daily basis, and the Kinder District staff was being less than helpful. There seemed to be only one option—to make Phil a focus of concern at Pride, finish out the year with him in place and then not renew his contact. But the Pride personnel director had a strong belief that doing this would allow Phil to go somewhere else and perhaps abuse future children. He decided to embarrass the Kinder District officials and the Kinder police. A lawsuit was prepared against both, and against Phil, claiming all had a duty to release information about Phil and the sledding incident. Then, rather than file the lawsuit, the Pride personnel director sent unfiled copies to each of the potential defendants suggesting that unless he had this report within a week, the suit would be filed.

The Kinder police were incensed, claiming that they were simply fulfilling their legal obligation to Phil and the victims as required by the State's Criminal Record Privacy Act, an act which protects the privacy of criminal suspects and victims. The Kinder District officials were equally incensed, claiming that their report to the police fulfilled all legal obligations and they were about to be unnecessarily humiliated. Phil retained his own lawyer, who claimed this lawsuit was entirely without merit and would result in a "massive" claim against Pride District. But, the Pride personnel director stayed the course and on the fifth day, the Kinder police decided to get in touch with the victim's mother and ask her what she wanted them to do. In the process, the Kinder police told the victim's mother where Phil was teaching, who the personnel director was, and how strongly Pride seemed to feel about the situation.

The mom, who hadn't known that Phil was teaching or even still living in the area, immediately got on the telephone to the Pride personnel director. She signed a release and the Pride personnel director got the police report from the Kinder police. He called Phil in to confront him with the new information; Phil had no explanation. He was then summarily dismissed, and the police report was turned over to the state certification authority. Shortly thereafter, Phil lost his certificate to teach. There was no lawsuit. All the threats against Pride ended. But Phil did not go away. A few weeks later, a Pride administrator reported seeing Phil officiating a Grid Kids football game between boys of fourth- through sixth-grade age.

Psychological Analysis

Once more we have the story of a physical education special-ist with a strong compulsion toward little boys. While we should not stereotype by teaching specialty, we must realize that opportunities for out-of-school contact and out-of-classroom activities maximize opportunities. Youthfulness and immaturity can motivate elementary age students to develop overly familial relationships with coaches.

Phil is single and lives alone. Habitation factors and age must be considered as potential risk factors affecting teacher assignment. Phil was instructed by his principal not to invite students to any sort of out-of-school activities. But he persisted. Compulsions are powerful urges to repeat behaviors even though the behaviors may be illogical or even criminal. We call them compulsions because people are compelled to commit these acts, even if doing them opposes their own well being. Once school officials realized that Phil was repeating exactly what he had been told not to do, Phil's teaching career suffered.

The principal responded well when he heard that Phil was inviting boys to extracurricular activities. However, when Phil persisted in planning camping activities, all Phil's actions, both in school and out of school, should have become suspicious. When Mary invited Phil to join her on the school trip, we realize that she may have invited the fox into the henhouse. It is Phil who needs chaperoning, not the little boys. But Mary was not aware of this when the offer was made.

Although Phil was not new to teaching, he was in his first year with this particular school district. He should have been treated as a "new employee" and should not have been trusted in the same way experienced teachers were trusted. Even though he was admonished to act and forego acting in various ways, he should have been followed more closely and been on a formal or informal probation. Also, when the school is choosing to offer out-of-school activities, the teacher in charge has to determine, in advance, whether or not parents are available to support the activity as chaperones rather than choosing to do the activity and then look for chaperones. Fathers should have been available; Mary never should have needed Phil in the first place.

The rest of the case illustrates the "pass the trash" syndrome which has existed for decades in school systems throughout the country. It seems more appropriate to many school administrators, and perhaps public prosecutors and parents, that if they can get the person out of the area the problem is somehow solved. Let the perpetrator leave—and soon! The fact that Phil is forty-years old, still has his teacher's credentials, and is not incarcerated may be directly related to this often followed mind-set. Phil has probably gotten away with incidents like the sledding many times before and therefore, he may have had many victims.

Children who become part of a trial as witnesses may be further victimized by participation in the legal proceedings. For that reason, many parents have chosen to avoid court in order to protect children who have already suffered abuse. In the process, the perpetrator gains an advantage. I do believe though that this process can further abuse a child. For example, the seven years that the McMartin Preschool students were involved in legal proceedings was probably not to their benefit. Still, the only way to stop the Phils of our world is to charge them, prosecute them, bar them from teaching, and make certain they receive treatment. This was not done by the previous school system. And, at the end of this case, we see that, in a non-school setting, Phil is still involved with little children.

Legal Analysis

Phil's story is an excellent example of how difficult it often is to get meaningful information about teachers. It is also an example of some of the rationalizations that school officials have historically used to excuse non-performance. Notice that there had been no "formal complaint," and there had been no "written complaint," but those are nothing more than shallow excuses for non-action. No one says that the boy's mother was told how to make a "formal complaint" and refused; no one says she was asked to make a "written complaint" and refused. In fact, she had made a "written complaint" to the police, and the school's disclaimer only referred to them not having a copy, which is the last thing they wanted to have to begin with! Phil was moved out of Kinder in a way that allowed him to compete for and get another job. Kinder facilitated the hope, believing that doing that would expedite his departure to another place—preferably one far, far away. However, that approach to this problem is no longer legally or ethically acceptable.

The principal in Kinder who wrote the recommendation for Phil while aware that he has possibly molested one of her students, violated the rights of other (future) students, and current law in many states allows those future students to sue her personally. Well it should. If not for her recommendation, Phil would not have been in a position to abuse, and society now attaches personal liability to this sort of misfeasance. Legally, the duty is now owed to *all* students, meaning an official of Kinder owes a duty not only to Kinder students but to students everywhere. In that same regard, note that Phil was last seen officiating a Grid Kids football game. Does this notice, this knowledge, now generate a duty on the part of Pride officials to notify the Grid Kids organization that Phil may be dangerous? We believe so. Actual notice of foreseeable risk to persons who are unable to protect themselves without full knowledge of the threat is, we believe, sufficient to impose that duty. Either report obvious risk or prepare to explain why you have chosen not to.

ADULT FEMALES AND MALE STUDENTS

Case 11: Sheila and Carl

Carl was a quiet, good looking, fifteen-year-old boy. He was somewhat self-assured. He seemed older than his fellow ninth graders. Carl had an unusual background. He had lived for a while in a car in the backyard of his uncle's house. He had no relationship with his father, and his mother was a drug addict. He says that he had always been sexually interested in girls and had his first intercourse when he was nine with a thirteen-year-old girl. He had continued to have sexual relationships during his early teenage years. He reported always feeling different than his peers since they were interested in sports and he was interested in sex.

As his ninth-grade year progressed, Carl's beloved grandfather died. He began a relationship with his art teacher, Sheila. She had invited him to her house to do chores, even though she had an eighteen-year old son living at home who could easily have done them. She bought Carl a bicycle and a leather bomber's jacket. Sheila would entertain men in her home, and Carl encountered men there. One weekend, Sheila asked Carl to help her put together a weight bench. During this activity, she asked him if he wanted to make love with her. Carl reported he was shocked. But fifteen minutes later, they made love. Over the next three months, Carl reported having intercourse with Sheila ten to twenty times. On at least one occasion, Carl reported that Sheila's son had driven him home after he had spent the night. Carl says that he spent a lot of time talking to Sheila. He could talk to her about his mother's addiction and about a previous girlfriend he had gotten pregnant. Once his affair with Sheila began, Carl gave up his other girlfriends, and although he says Sheila said she loved him, he reported not being sure he loved Sheila. According to Carl, the relationship ended as their passion cooled. He then met a fifteen-year-old girl, Nita, and began seeing her. After four months, Carl had sexual intercourse with Nita and she developed genital herpes, which she attributed to having had sex with him. Carl then confronted Sheila and she denied ever having herpes. Nita was in a great deal of pain, and Carl, allegedly angry with Sheila, went to the police.

Carl became locally famous. He developed insomnia. His grades nose-dived. At one time, he was asked to appear on a day-time talk show and got an expense-paid trip to New York. Eventually, some four years later, as a result of a civil suit against the school district, he received $70,000. After graduating from high school with "Cs" and "Ds," he became more and more depressed. He had a lot of anger toward Sheila and felt his troubles would constantly follow him. At one time, he made a weak suicide attempt by overdosing on his sister's epilepsy medicine. He then met and married his current wife. This relationship was up and down over the next couple of years, during which he worked at a pet store and then a restaurant. Then there was another suicide attempt. Eventually, his wife became pregnant and they had a son. Both he and his wife now take medication for depression. Presently, at age twenty-five, he seems dedicated to his wife and child and is working hard to pull his life together.

Sheila was thirty-eight at the time of her liaison with Carl.

She was divorced and lived with her eighteen-year-old son. Earlier in her adult years, she had been a medical technician and had also worked as a waitress in a restaurant. She had been a teacher for several years. In her previous school district, she had been president of the local education association. Two years before her liaison with Carl, she had testified, as a district witness, at the dismissal hearing of another teacher charged with sexually abusing fifth-grade girls; she had testified to this teacher having told her he had abused a babysitter and how he had been abused by co-workers in a lumber mill. At the time of her affair with Carl, Sheila was a remarkably attractive woman who enjoyed the company of several local men her age who were financially successful and socially prominent in the community. Both at home and at school, Sheila tended to dress and act as if she were in her late teens or early twenties. Although she had not worked as a public school administrator, she had earned her principal's credentials. In the course of earning those credentials, she had studied laws and regulations pertaining to child abuse and child sexual abuse in public schools. Sheila was not a person who should have known better—she knew what she was doing was wrong.

When Carl's claims first arose, Sheila denied them. Later, she pleaded guilty to statutory rape in the third degree and told the pre-sentence investigator that she and Carl had "sexual intercourse and oral sex on ten to twenty occasions in her home and in her car." Asked how many times at each location, she replied, "I don't recall; I wasn't keeping score." On at least one occasion, when Sheila and Carl had sexual intercourse at her home, Sheila's son, who was older than Carl, was also present in the home.

After the events described above, Sheila moved away and established herself in another Pacific Northwest community. She gave up her teaching certificate and is now pursuing a career in respiratory therapy. As this is written, Sheila is engaged to be married—to a man her own age.

The sexual incidents had occurred between February and June, 1987. All had occurred away from school, but there were events at school that raised concern. To begin with, Sheila and

Carl were repeatedly observed dancing close at the school's Valentine's Day dance. This dance had immediately preceded the first sexual contacts. About this time, the assistant principal later reported that he had become very concerned about Sheila's relationship with Carl saying, "Carl was spending a great deal of time with Sheila after school in her room. Sometimes other students would be present, and sometimes they would be alone. Carl was Sheila's teaching assistant second semester in one of her art classes. The assistant principal later said, "I observed her dancing a slow dance with Carl with her arms around his neck and his arms around her waist. . . . [The principal] and I met with Sheila in the spring to discuss her professional behavior. We cautioned her not to become too friendly with students and not to put herself in a position that could be misinterpreted. We discussed the dances, having students in her room, and giving students rides home."

Psychological Analysis

Carl is a young man who has had to grow up quickly. Like many street children, in some ways he is older than his years. In other ways, these precocious children are deficient in moral development. Having to survive on their own, they tend to satisfy their own needs without concern for right and wrong. Carl was drawn into an enjoyable and profitable relationship with a teacher that many other students desired. He had a sexual background and was not afraid of sex. He also had no adult to confide in, and that became part of his relationship with Sheila. Clearly, he enjoyed the benefits of their liaison until his passion cooled.

His roving eye led him to Nita. It was only when he became angry with Sheila and felt deceived by her that he decided to blow the whistle on her. Clearly, his psychological problems both predate and postdate Sheila. She should have recognized the dangers, both personally and professionally, of being involved with Carl, who is still suffering because of the relationship. It is very difficult for a teenage boy to turn down a sexual request from an attractive adult female.

Sheila was clearly a case of arrested maturity. Her dress and style attest to her desire to remain youthful and desirable. She enjoyed being different from the other teachers. For example, she regularly enjoyed "X"-rated movies and made no secret of it. Her sexual passion drove her toward men and boys. Since all her conquests were postpubescent, she was not a pedophile but she was a TSAS. Sheila did not concern herself with the effects on her students or her representativeness of the teaching profession. She did not control her behavior, even after her conversations with the principal and assistant principal.

Legal Analysis

I recall when Carl's claims first came to light and I was interviewing him, his foster brothers, and foster mother. I wondered then and wonder now about his reporting on Sheila only after their passion cooled. An associate of mine summed it up well, saying, "Why kill Santa Claus?" I felt at the time and feel now that Sheila broke off the relationship and Carl continued to lust after her, and once it was apparent that she was not going to continue to fulfill his sexual needs, he attacked her by bringing formal charges against her. During that period, for some months, I believe he knew he had genital herpes. I do, incidentally, believe Sheila gave it to him, but I also believe he continued to see himself in love with her after that, and based upon the later history Dr. Rubin presents above, he may still feel he is in love with her.

These are the most difficult cases to ferret out. When I investigated this case, I focused on Carl's fellow students, feeling confident that Carl would brag of his conquest of Sheila, but he never did. Apparently, the relationship was valuable enough to him that he knew it was best not to brag and thus run the risk of offending Sheila or exposing the relationship. I found no peer, including his foster brothers, who knew he was having sexual relations with Sheila. Interestingly though, I did find he bragged about sexual conquests of girls his own age.

Similarly, I looked at Sheila's adult associates (friends) and wondered if they had not seen events at home that administrators could not identify at school and I felt I found one. She would not admit her factual basis but did admit that she had counseled Sheila to break off the ostensible yard-boy–teacher relationship with Carl. Ironically, I believe Sheila grudgingly followed this friend's advice, thus leading to Carl, with broken heart, reporting her.

I don't doubt that Sheila knew that what she was doing was highly improper. This was not a "should have known" case; she knew. Also, the building administrators counseled her and she denied the relationship. Certainly, in retrospect, the point where the administration failed its duty was there. Sheila should not have been believed. An investigation should then have been started. A long time ago, an old country lawyer told me, "Never trust anyone, including the client." That was good advice then, and it is good advice to school administrators today.

The investigation should have been done by an independent investigator—not the building administrator, who was responsible for allowing the relationship to blossom at school. Here, the administrator questioning Sheila and Carl was acting as an investigator. He was inclined to wish the whole mess would go away. When the formal investigation was done, in part, it was an investigation of the administrators. I know because I did that investigation. I also know that the responsible building administrator was rightfully concerned about his career because, as a result of my investigation and Carl's charges against Sheila, that administrator lost his principalship and has not had one since.

Point–Counterpoint

Psychologist: Our society is struggling with the double standard. Are women equal to men and as culpable and as responsible for their experiences? I believe that we should hold adult women to the same standard as adult men. Not only should Sheila have lost her certificate, she should have been prosecuted for statutory rape. She took advantage of a disturbed adolescent, causing him grief. She did this with a full awareness of what she was doing. Certainly she has problems that need treatment. Her colleagues should have done more to prevent the relationship. Perhaps they too thought that they should not kill "Santa Claus"; perhaps all of us feel that a fifteen-year-old boy engaging in a sexual relationship with a female teacher is not as wrong as a fifteen-year-old girl engaging in a sexual relationship with a male teacher. As a psychologist, I do feel that these are different situations, but this does not mean that it is good for either of the participants. The relationship can only cause problems and the school is not set up as a sexual therapeutic community. This is not sex education.

Attorney: I agree. Our laws require that the treatment of culpable adults be gender neutral. Even so, Sheila was not treated as severely as a male teacher would probably have been in the same circumstances. She was placed on probation and given community service for a few weeks. That is not particularly important to me and should not be to you either. My greatest concern is that this situation may be perceived as so exceptional it is not worthy of educational community concern. That is not my experience. In my career I have dealt with five cases involving adult women and postpubescent males of student age, one involving an adult female staff person and several older prepubescent boys. These cases do occur and I have found them to be the most difficult to investigate and the most difficult to end.

In my experience, these relationships have presented when the female staff person wanted pictures with the boy or pictures of the boy, was offering rides to or from school or home, was offering yardwork (as here), or was offering outings or volunteering to act as an adult supervisor on outings. These circumstances need to be considered suspicious events. Administrators must challenge these events asking, "What is the educational purpose?" When that purpose is not apparent, action must be taken to wind up the non-educational aspects of the relationship. That ought to involve serious consideration of involuntary transfer of the adult female employee to a worksite away from the student. The student's right to an educational environment free of sexual exploitation should always take precedence over employment rights of the teacher. That rule ought to be rigidly applied whether the offending adult is a man or a woman.

Case 12: Mary and Steve

Mary was a thirty-five-year-old, highly regarded, sixth-grade teacher and mother of four who gave birth to a daughter fathered by a thirteen-year-old student. At the time of this relationship, Mary had four children, some of whom were older than her lover. She had been raised in a strict Catholic household in southern California. She had, however, been moved from one private Catholic school to another because her father felt that the schools were "getting too liberal."

Her father, a John Birch Society member, championed keeping sex education out of the schools. Politically, he was anti-Semitic, anti-black, and anti-feminist. He had a colorful political career and was elected to the state senate several times. Eventually, his career ended when it was discovered that he had engaged in numerous extramarital affairs and, during his marriage to Mary's mother, had fathered illegitimate children.

The case became public when Mary's husband told someone that he thought that his wife was pregnant with the boy's child and then told the authorities. Mary was suspended by her employing school district, and criminal court proceedings were deferred while she awaited the birth of the child she was carrying. Mary's union with the boy produced a child of mixed race, the racial mix alone conclusively proving the child was not fathered by her husband and was, in fact, fathered by the student. After the child was born, Mary's husband filed for divorce and thereafter, based upon her unfitness to mother the children, he was awarded custody of the couple's other four children. He then moved with the children to another state. Mary is now in prison and her life as a mother, wife, and successful teacher is a shambles.

Mary had been the boy's second-grade teacher and later, his sixth grade teacher. Her relationship with him became sexual during the summer of his sixth-grade year. Following her release from jail, Mary was probationed on condition she have no contact with the boy, a condition she chose to ignore. She is now pregnant with her second child by the boy. Instead of the suspended sentence, community treatment and probation ordered after the first instance, she is now serving a minimum seven year prison sentence. The father of these children is still in middle school.

Psychological Analysis

Mary is a seemingly successful woman with a large family and an ongoing teaching career. It is difficult to understand how her relationship with Steve could have become sexual. As he entered puberty, he may have developed sexual needs. Perhaps Mary saw her role as teacher as including teaching

Steve about sex. Steve may have become a confidant with whom she could talk about her unhappy marriage. Perhaps he talked to her about his pubescent urges. Verbal intimacy can become physical intimacy as many counselors and therapists have sadly discovered. It is difficult to understand how Mary could allow herself to become pregnant unless she had a powerful need to have children. Of course, the pregnancy may merely have been accidental. The communication between Mary and her husband had probably been poor for some time. Mary's inability to control herself, knowing the risks that she was taking, suggests both the power of her desire for this boy and the confusion/disturbance she demonstrates. According to her husband, Mary described the boy as a "gifted artist," saying that she still loves him. He found love letters from his wife to the boy and was in denial until he actually found them asleep together. Mary's husband now reports that their children are confused and depressed. It is clear that the word *victim* could be applied to Mary's husband and children.

Mary's case clearly demonstrates just how irrational the TSAS situation is. It need not be a case of a lonely, frustrated, teacher/spinster clutching at a young man. In this case and the earlier case of the junior high art teacher (Case 11), we see that an attractive, successful, even married woman can become so confused that she can cross the line from teacher to lover. This can occur not just with a seventeen- or eighteen-year-old young man but a thirteen-year-old boy. Somehow, these "mature," successful women can deny the laws, deny the reality, and cognitively distort the situation.

In sex offender treatment lingo they convince themselves, through cognitive distortions or "stinking thinking" that their relationship with these young boys is OK. They rationalize and become unconcerned with the consequences to all those involved, such as the family members of both families. A delusion is developed that greatly distorts the motives, benefits, and harms involved.

It is unknown whether any teachers or friends noticed the developing odd relationship that Mary had, but at some point her husband did. What is his responsibility to the school district or to Steve's family? There was probably no way for the school district to "screen out" Mary when she applied to teach. Were there any continuing education programs focused on the destructiveness of sexual relations between students and staff? Were there any warnings from the administration? These issues might speak to the issue of civil liability. Did Steve's parents notice any unusual relationship between him and this teacher? Were there any discussions with school officials during the years of growing intimacy between Steve and Mary?

There is increasing evidence, mostly case by case, of the destructiveness of these boy–women affairs. It appears not to be healthy for the "lucky" young man. It probably causes confusion and greatly distorts the normal developmental stage of adolescent romance. At a time when the debate between sex as a recreational past time and sex as part of a committed relationship is critically joined, the TSAS situation adds just one more piece of evidence to those who say, "Just Do It." Don't be concerned with hurting others, follow your heart and "love" will conquer all—whatever that means.

Legal Analysis

As a general rule, someone under the age of fourteen cannot *legally* assume risk, or consent. In particular, someone under fourteen cannot "consent" to a sexual relationship. Instead, society rightly assumes that the participant, boy or girl, is too immature to fully appreciate the consequences of sexual intercourse. Here, the sexual intercourse is not only with an adult, the adult is more than five years older than the child and was in a real position of authority over the child. Clearly, this is an adult who exploited the teacher–student relationship, an act akin to a bank officer violating a fiduciary obligation and embezzling his employer's money, but this is much worse.

I cannot imagine how school staff could be unaware of the *possibility* of an abusive relationship here. I cannot believe that fellow teachers could be unaware of the *possibility* of an abusive relationship here. I cannot believe that Steve's friends, both boys and girls, were not suspicious. This sort of situation is inexcusable. Everyone has a duty to report child abuse. That includes Mary's spouse, her co-workers and anyone else who has reasonable cause to believe that abuse is occurring. Some of the persons in those categories failed to fulfill their duty to society in general and to Steve in particular.

The school district is held to the standard of "knew or should have known" and thus contentions that administrators did not know are legally irrelevant. The standard is "should have known" and the boy and his parents should have little difficulty proving to a jury that school officials "should have known." Usually, the only substantive issues in this sort of situation revolve around just what it is school officials "should have known." In general, attorneys for the school district will argue that there is insufficient proof that officials "should have known" of an intimate relationship, and attorneys for the child and his parents will argue that school officials "should have known" information sufficient to raise concerns—information sufficient to impose a duty to look further and, if the relationship had been strictly scrutinized, school officials would have interrupted it.

Note that the sexual relationship apparently did not even begin until the school year ended. Thus, during that sexual relationship, over the summer, Mary was technically not even a teacher for the school district or Steve's teacher. She was between contracts. Nonetheless, in my opinion, school officials "should have known" of a familial relationship between Mary and Steve that had no apparent educational purpose. Apparently this relationship, which predated the sexual relationship, had been ongoing for some time. School officials focusing on this relationship should have at least separated Mary and Steve and admonished Mary to avoid associations with him.

We need to recognize however that the relationship between Mary and Steve was so bizarre it was extremely difficult to deal with. As we move toward the cusp of the unimaginable, the amount of proof necessary to prove the issue increases. Thus, the proof necessary to create a foreseeable risk of an overly familial relationship between Mary and an eighteen-year-old Steve is less than that necessary to support a foreseeable risk of relationship between Mary and a twelve- or thirteen-year-old Steve. Add Mary's stable marriage and four children, some older than Steve, and many people literally have to see the two in bed together to believe it; the husband, for example, did not report it until he caught them in bed together. Therefore, it is easy to retrospectively criticize, but difficult to deal with, a relationship of this sort in the present. However, society rightly criticizes and does not care whether Mary's supervising administrators were culpable, or naive, or just plain dumb; in this sort of situation, society, by its court system, imposes a form of strict liability. As a result, over a period of time, future children in Steve's situation will find the relationship interrupted before it goes as far as the relationship did here.

CHAPTER 4

Psychological and Emotional Causes— Teachers Who Sexually Abuse Students

THE PSYCHOLOGIST'S PERSPECTIVE[1]

WE know that most teachers do not cross the line and become sexually involved with students. However some do, and in order to assist in identifying these persons before they abuse, K–12 administrators must have some appreciation for the abuser's psyche. First, we present a general profile and then focus, in particular, on teachers.

Behavior is the function of the situation and the person. By this, I mean that people in different situations act differently, and different people in the same situation act differently. For example, people growing up in Aspen, Colorado, learn to ski and people growing up in Malibu, California, learn to surf, and often the best explanation for what people do is found in the situation that they are in. As a result, when I am in front of a college classroom I act like a professor, but when I am in an audience listening to a visiting scholar I act more like a student. Thus, most (but not all) of our behavior can be predicted if we understand the situation "press," as Henry Murray called it.

The other large group of determining factors relates to the "person" or "person variables." In summary, people are different and those individual differences allow us to predict their behavior in various situations. For example, compulsively neat people will have neat offices, cars, and even neat garages. If they are camping, they will even have a neat tent!

[1]This section is authored by Dr. Rubin.

Our general explanation of human behavior, in summary, is that people act the way they do as a result of a combination of both the situations they are in *and* who they are as people. But, there is a qualifier: It may not be the situation that they are in so much as the situation that they *believe they are in* that is determinative. As cognizant beings we attempt to assess and figure out our situations before we act. In the process, it is our awareness of the situation rather than the situation itself that is crucial.

Consider the individual differences between us and how we come to be the sexual people that we are. There are different theoretical explanations for our sexual interests. Freud suggested that all of us progress through psychosexual stages. At different stages we normally are drawn to different areas of the body and different activities. For instance, during the earliest stage, the oral stage, we interact with the world through our mouth. Sucking, swallowing, licking, and eventually talking are the favored activities. These activities retain some of their erotic value as we mature, hence many adults enjoy kissing, licking, oral sex, and even talking erotically. Similarly, anal and phallic activities retain erotic value for many of us. These too were infantile activities of major interest early in our lives. The hallmark of adult, genital sexuality for the mature individual is the desire to have intercourse with the adult of the opposite sex. All the "immature" activities, including desires for children or desires for the same sex, become secondary or merely foreplay. Most, but not all of us, grow out of our sexual immaturity.

According to classic psychoanalytic theory, pedophiles, exhibitionists, voyeurs, and even homosexuals are sexually immature. Groth (1979) popularized the dichotomy dividing rapists into two groups: fixated and regressed. Groth theorized that the fixated group of rapists was "stuck" at a certain psychosexual stage and hence continued to seek the behaviors and partners that they had always found sexually satisfying. Thus, if "playing doctor" was an enjoyable game with peers at age six, then it might continue to be enjoyable to this sort of person for the rest of his life. The regressed offender, on the other hand, is one who, because of the stress and dissatisfaction of unsatisfactory sexual experiences as an adult, attempts to return to the sexual satisfaction enjoyed or imagined as a child. These are persons who have grown up and grown beyond pre-genital sexuality but, at times, attempt to return to the pleasures of childhood.

Although, like most theorists, he did not write about them, Groth's theory helps us understand the teacher who sexually abuses students. If we more carefully investigate the sexual and relationship backgrounds of prospective teachers, we might be able to identify some who do not appear to have made a mature progression through the psychosexual stages.

There are, however, real problems with Freud's underlying theory. That homosexuality is a fixation or manifestation of immature sexual development, or a sign of psychological disturbance, has now been disproved. It is now generally recognized that homosexuality, by itself, is not evidence of psychological disturbance. By itself, homosexuality is not generally considered a risk factor for pedophilia, and most child molesters are not homosexuals. Also, teachers who sexually abuse students fall into two general categories; they are rapists or pedophiles. In most cases, the victims are not *biologically immature* and hence, by definition, the abusing teacher is not a pedophile. Also, in most cases, *aggression and power* are not the issue and so the abusing teachers are not rapists. There is less evidence of aggression and hostility in the typical abusing teacher and more evidence of unfulfilled love and sexual needs being fulfilled in a situation wherein the teacher exerts some power over the victim. Enjoyment of power is likely one of the motives for some people in choosing the teaching profession. Perhaps, as Sgroi (1982) says, all child molesters are acting out as a result of power needs, not sexual needs.

In a chapter in *The Juvenile Sex Offender* Bukowski, Sippola, and Brender (1993) review sexual development concepts and argue that normal development requires the integration of one's sense of self and relationships within the cultural context. They remind us that understanding one's sexuality requires understanding the resolution of the self/other dialect as well as integrating one's needs. Taking a developmental perspective, they suggest that sexuality changes depending on where the individual is in his or her life process. Thus, while behaviors may appear similar, the meanings of those behaviors may be very different if the participants' ages are different. For example, intercourse between a thirty-five-year-old teacher and a twelve-year-old student probably is the product of very different motivations than the motivations leading to a relationship between a sixty-year-old teacher and a fourteen-year-old student, or the relationship between a twenty-four-year-old teacher and a sixteen-year-old student. As a result, it is perhaps unfair to attempt to treat those various associations by the same general standards.

In *The Juvenile Sex Offender* Abel, Osborne, and Twiggy (1993) also quickly review three predominant theories regarding development of sexual deviations. In summary, the psychoanalytic-fixation theory proposes that the adult offender is developmentally impaired; the cognitive model suggests that the adult offender develops unusual thought patterns, such as reaching the conclusion that "teaching the child (the victim) about sex will help her grow up." The resulting behavior then follows from the cognitive distortion. Finally, the conditioning model, they explain, is the one in which the sexual behavior becomes associated with and reinforced by the eventual pleasure produced (the orgasm) and frequent reinforcement operates to sustain the deviant behavior over many years. In reviewing various theories, Marshall, Hudson, and Hodkinson (1993) say that "A comprehensive theory of sex offending is probably not possible. We need to develop specific theories for each type of offense that emphasize different processes" (p. 137).

With the foregoing in mind, we now focus on teachers. No previous books have had this particular focus, and the individual sex offenders within this group may not be typical of persons who sexually abuse children. For example, all teachers may be drawn to a position of power over the young people who are their students, and most students who are abused by teachers are not prepubertal; though legally considered children, the typical female student victim is a sexually mature young lady who is abused by a mature male teacher. Since our culture is youth oriented, teachers who spend their time around young men and young women are following a strong, normal, cultural trend. The child victim usually is acting out this trend by trying out her sexuality at an increasingly younger age and, because most teachers who sexually abuse students focus their attention on postpubescent children rather than prepubescent children, most are not pedophiles.

Although the teacher–student relationship is particularly attractive to certain people, not all adults want to become teachers, and some that choose teaching later question that choice. Teachers receive particular sorts of psychological rewards. They enjoy the love and admiration of their students. They believe that they are helping students to be successful. They usually enjoy teaching their particular subject to students. Some enjoy the position of power over students and a few enjoy flirting with the students. All teachers do not have the same psychological needs or derive the same psychological benefits. As the teacher journeys through his or her adult life and teaching career, the teaching profession often fulfills and/or frustrates needs differently at different ages.

The current, generally accepted psychological theory for explaining human behavior is the cognitive-social-learning theory. The earlier Psychoanalytic model argued that the intrapsychic, psychosexual factors caused character development and that adult behavior was both consciously and unconsciously caused by intrapsychic forces, such as repressed, aggressive, or sexual needs. Then, Behaviorism said that our behaviors were controlled by the consequences of those behaviors. We would behave in ways for which we had been rewarded. Our present and previous environments controlled what we did. It now seems that both extreme theoretical positions overstated the evidence.

The current formulation, the Cognitive-Social-Learning Theory, supports the idea that all of us think somewhat differently, and that our thinking influences our behavior and vice versa. Further, our history of reward shapes our thinking, like our behavior. In addition, we control our situations, and the situations that we find ourselves in ideally influence but sometimes control us.

Bandura (1977) theorized that the reinforcers in our environment, our cognitions and our sense of self, all are categories of variables related to our behavior. In practice, this means that there are differences between teachers in both behavior and in thinking. There are small minorities of teachers who are pedophiles and another larger group who are sexually attracted to young postpubescent adults. These groups of individuals become teachers because of their sexual needs and look for opportunities to be sexual with students. These are the predators. Yet there is another and even larger subset of TSAS who are neither pedophiles nor predators; these teachers are people who, at some time in some situations, develop distorted thoughts and make poor choices that lead to inappropriate sexual contact with students.

David Finkelhor, an expert on child molesters, focuses on four key factors: emotional congruence, sexual arousal to children, blockage, and disinhibition (1984). Finkelhor believes that some adults are more comfortable with and can have their emotional needs met by children. He reports that while some adults demonstrate a high level of sexual arousal to children, many demonstrate different arousal patterns but do not necessarily act on those feelings. By "blockage," Finkelhor means that some adults are blocked in their ability to get their emotional needs met by adult relationships (which is akin to the "fixated" offender described in earlier theory). "Disinhibition" raises the issue of why offenders do not have the moral or behavioral stopgaps to control their sexual feelings towards children. Alcohol abuse, lack of sufficient social mores in some societal subgroups, and common cognitive distortions might explain this. For example, when people drink they become disinhibited. A teacher who tells himself that having sex with a thirteen-year-old is part of sex education is typically disinhibited (cognitive distortions like this do occur in sex offenders). In my opinion, Finkelhor's multi-factor theory is an important improvement on the earlier theory. The theory's one weakness, as I see it, is failure to focus enough attention on the powerful situational determinants common to our society. This is a particular weakness when the multi-factor theory is applied to incidents of child molestation within the teaching profession.

If behavior is a function of the combination of the personality of the teacher and the situation, then we must learn more about whom we hired and what situations are risky for that person. By situation, I mean the classroom or teaching setting, the attitudes, the student characteristics, including the student age and maturity level, the place, the time, and the quality of teacher–student interactions. Very simply, a teacher drawn to a particular age, gender, and personality type of student ought not be in a non-supervised situation with that type of student. I believe most teacher–student sexual relations can be understood by looking at the people involved and the situations that they are involved in. Teacher–student interactions that occur off-campus, or which are intensely emotional or solitary events, are dangerous situations. In my 1988 national survey (Rubin, 1988), I found that most cases involved coaches, music teachers, art instructors, homeroom teachers, and counselors. These are often gregarious, outgoing personality types or persons in an intimate or familial relationship with the student. I found that emotionally needy or precociously sexual students are more prone to be victimized. When these personality types are combined, and when the teachers have unfulfilled needs—for example a desire to be "youthful," and who elect to spend an inordinate amount of time with students, the students are at risk. School systems without careful training and clear guidelines regarding teacher–student interactions may be leaving too much to chance, meaning that without clear, unambiguous guidelines and specified rules, too many choices are left to the teacher and student.

In many of the cases in which we have become involved, we find a bond or attachment between the abusing teacher and the abused student. Marshall, Hudson and Hodkinson (1993), in *The Juvenile Sex Offender* discuss that bonding process. It is very possible that teachers who become involved with students suffer from underlying attachment problems that lead to and motivate these destructive relationships. The vulnerable student may be seeking a relationship because of a history of loneliness and abuse. Today's students are the product of a society marked by rampant divorce, reconstituted families, single and "latch-key" parents, and generally strange and often fluid home environments. Both modern teachers and modern students are likely to be attachment needy. Together, these factors suggest that sexual contact alone may not be the major motivator in all teacher–student abuse cases.

In summary, our explanation for teachers who sexually abuse students revolves around two types of abusers: first, the predatory pedophile or teacher focused on postpubescent young adults, and second, the situational offender. Both can be explained by the type of people involved and the situations they are involved in. The steps that school systems and parents can take to prevent future crimes from occurring are different and will be discussed in the chapter on prevention. As stated by Becker, Alpert, Bigfoot, and Walker (1955), "There is no empirically derived and universally agreed-on model to explain why some individuals molest children and others go on to develop the paraphernalia of pedophilia."

We still must proceed on what is presently our best theory. And, we must recognize that we will inevitably learn more than we know now.

A more complicated theory, but one that helps explain some TSAS, relates to the combination of attachment and intimacy. Ward, Hudson, Marshall, and Siegert (1995) use Bowlby's theory of attachment and Bartholomew's theory of adult intimacy needs to differentiate between sex offenders. Bowlby's lifework focused on the initial bonds between children and parents. He and other English psychoanalysts wrote about three types of attachments: secure, insecure, and ambivalent. Bartholomew (1990) and Bartholomew and Horowitz (1991) broadened this theory into four types of adult attachment: secure, anxious/ambivalent, and two types of avoidant styles. His understanding is that adults have an internal model of the self and an internal model of others. Each of these models has positive and negative valences and hence, there are four attachment styles. An adult sees him or herself as worthy or unworthy of love and others as either trustworthy or available or unreliable and rejecting. The three non-secure attachment styles predict different types of offender–victim relationships.

As Feeny and Noller (1990) and Hazen and Shaver (1994) pointed out, anxious/ambivalently attached individuals are more concerned with relationships, fall in love easily, and experience extreme emotional states. They need approval and, as Ward et al. (1995) explained, the child whom they can control and who admires them makes them feel secure. These are needy children who come out of their own insecure childhoods in search of a loving, secure relationship. The offender who interacts with them, whether a teacher or not, finds security and affection through sexual interactions, and consequently the children are powerfully sexualized. Clearly, this theory rests on the assumption that human behavior is not often based on carefully thought out choices which consider consequences, but on powerful unconscious and unresolved needs.

The attachment/intimacy topology will be useful as we develop a system of characterizing TSAS. By taking Ward et al.'s theory (1995) further and applying it to teachers we will, I believe, commonly see teachers who present as "Avoidant I" personalities—persons who desire close contact and are afraid of rejection. To them, sexual contact is an indirect means of making contact. The sexual contact is impersonal, and this personality type consequently exhibits little guilt. Alternatively, the "Avoidant II" personality, commonly found among child molesters in general, presents with more hostility and aggression and blames others for a lack of intimacy.

Given the foregoing theories, research, and general considerations, we begin with a broad dichotomy between pedophiles and non-pedophiles.

Pedophiles: In the educational setting, these are TSAS whose *primary* sexual interest is in prepubescent children. They present with chronic fantasies of young children. Their history shows an ongoing conflict between desire and control. Their focus was fixated early, and although their history of sexual relationships might include adults, their primary target has not wavered. They may be homosexual, heterosexual, or bisexual. They become teachers because of their interest in prepubescent children.

Non-pedophiles: Again, this is the largest group of TSAS. They are not sexually interested in biologically prepubescent children and thus act out sexually against pubescent or postpubescent students. Their victims, while legally considered children (under age eighteen) are, biologically, young adults.

As we explore the adult relationships of these teachers we see that they are often hungry for love, intimacy, and companionship. They often exhibit a dearth of healthy adult relationships or a multitude of shallow adult relationships. They tend to spend extensive time with students. Their relationship/intimacy needs often get them into trouble as they, so to speak, "look for love in all the wrong places."

According to Bartholomew (1990), a more careful analysis will often find nuances and subsets of relationship needs. For example, their behaviors in the school setting might be characterized by flirting, palling around with students, non-professional verbalizations (use of four letter words), and an inappropriately easygoing attitude with the students. This attitude may tend to create a positive, informal, and friendly teacher–student relationship. But, unfortunately, because not all teachers can draw the line between mere informality and inappropriate behavior, this attitude may also, sadly, lead into the dark corridors of sexual abuse.

Not all teachers can draw the line between informality and inappropriateness, and this may (see J. Biggs's comments following this section) become the school attorney's worst nightmare. In recent years, the line between informality and inappropriateness has become even more obscured by the emergence of gender-based sexual harassment issues. Within that concept, what is funny and friendly to twenty-nine students in a class may be onerous and litigious to a few students or even one student. Within these crosscurrents, an experienced pedophile may use language and incidental contact as coordinated steps in a purposefully deepening relationship with a chosen victim. Meanwhile, the non-pedophile TSAS may be enjoying the informal, friendly fooling around and not see the danger. At what point then do colleagues or administrators say something to the friendly, time-committing, teacher-of-the-year candidate? He or she is not a pedophile acting out a preplanned assault. What is occurring is not grooming, it is a flirtatious, informal repartee, but one which can, if left unchecked, become dangerous both to students and to the teacher. Therefore, the school system must take steps to guarantee, as much as possible, not to make something more than what it is.

While no one wants the schools to become impersonal and cold, we must become more aware and more proactive in recognizing that some teachers and some students, because of their intimacy needs, cannot handle informal flirting. They need guidelines, controls, and policing.

As a psychologist, I see the distinction between the pedophile and the non-pedophile as paramount. While both may become physically intimate with students, the pedophile is driven to repeat these acts. Teaching is not the place for a person with the sexual compulsions of a pedophile. He/she needs incarceration and extensive treatment if he/she is ever to be allowed full partnership in our communities. The non-pedophile TSAS, however, needs help. Because he/she is not driven by the same compulsions and is therefore not as dangerous as the pedophile, I believe that use of suspension, treatment, education, and firm controls can salvage the non-pedophile TSAS's career. This sort of person is and can continue to be responsible for his actions, but I believe that parents, students, and an indifferent atmosphere in the school system may have contributed to the abuse, and thus permitted his/her behavior to occur. I recognize, however (see comments of J. Biggs, following), that school attorneys will often disagree.

THE SCHOOL ATTORNEY'S REJOINDER[2]

To begin, I do not doubt Dr. Rubin's research or his conclusions as to cause. In general, he identifies the indicia of the pedophile, then the non-pedophile TSAS. Within this latter category, he recognizes that there are both compulsive persons who focus attention on biologically mature students who may be as young as thirteen or fourteen and thus are immature adults, and persons who are good teachers incapable of maintaining the proper teacher–student distinction and who, as a result, end up sexually involved with a student. He recognizes that we have to exercise even greater efforts to get the pedophiles out of K–12 education and keep them out. He recognizes that the incorrigible teacher who interacts sexually with im-

[2]This section is authored by Mr. Biggs.

mature teenage students also must be removed. But, as to the teacher who unintentionally finds him or herself sexually and emotionally involved, Dr. Rubin advocates retention and he does so because he sees the misbehaving teacher, the student(s), their parents, and the school system *sharing responsibility*. As a psychologist, his focus is first on motivation and causation, and secondarily on effect. To him, the cup is half full.

To me, the cup is half empty. As a school attorney, my focus is on effect. If a student has been sexually abused, I do not much care whether the teacher is a pedophile or a non-pedophile TSAS, or whether that teacher groomed and planned a seduction or, with the best of intentions, found him or herself involved sexually with a student. I see a student who has been abused, a person who has done the abusing, and my first reaction is to remove the abuser from the school system.

I follow a simple credo: First, I protect the student; next, I protect the employee; and finally, I protect the educational process. When retention of an employee heightens risk to kids, the employee is removed. But, when we deal with someone who has very little instructional skill or classroom management, for example, but who is not a danger to students, I err on the side of retention, recognizing that by doing so, the educational process is weakened by retention of a marginal teacher. Dr. Rubin, regarding the TSAS who can (in his opinion) be rehabilitated, raises that person's retention to the same level as the student's right to a healthful educational atmosphere and thus, believing that the risk of recurrence is slight, advocates retention of the employee. I do not agree. To me, a modest foreseeable risk and a clearly foreseeable risk are both risks to student health, safety, and welfare and should be avoided. Therefore, I continue to attempt to remove teachers who sexually abuse students.

With the qualifiers stated following, I concede Dr. Rubin's general point. If our focus is on protecting *all* kids twenty-four hours a day, 365 days a year, retaining some of these persons makes sense. But if our focus is on protecting students at school during the school year, retaining them makes no sense. When I am successful in ridding K–12 education of one of these people, he or she does not go to Mars. They generally stay in the community and continue to be drawn to kids. If sick and if a danger to kids yesterday, they are generally just as sick and at least as dangerous tomorrow. Since they cannot be around kids at school, they become lifeguards in swimming pools, "Grid Kids" coaches or referees, Cub or Boy Scout or Brownie leaders, church youth leaders, choir directors, etc. They become harder to monitor, and rehabilitation becomes less likely.

The school system that rids itself of one of these people has improved the safety of the educational environment at school, but probably made the community environment even more dangerous. I say that, because contrary to Dr. Rubin's supposition, not all of the pedophiles and non-pedophiles focused on abuse of immature adults are incarcerated. Most are either not incarcerated at all or incarcerated for brief periods of time. They are often young enough to present a danger to kids for decades to come.

Therefore, while I believe we have to continue to exercise best efforts to keep them out of K–12 education to begin with, I can see some merit in retaining them within K–12 after they have abused. However, I believe that can only be done when and if the education associations (unions) representing the aberrant employee are legally tasked with the responsibility to ensure no recurrence. To me, that is essential because without it, no administrator who plans to continue a career in public education should give serious consideration to retention. A change in current law is, in my opinion, a precondition to acceptance of Dr. Rubin's position.

The following news story presents a classic example:

Lincoln High teacher sued for sexual harassment

Two former students are suing the Tacoma School District and a Lincoln High School teacher on charges he sexually harassed them while they were in school.

Kelly—and Larissa—, now 20, state . . . Parker made sexual advances and comments toward them between 1991 and 1994, when they were minors. . . . The suit also names former Lincoln principal Charlie—, alleging he and the district failed to appropriately deal with the charges against Parker, a math teacher and former team trainer for girls sports. . . .

In the lawsuit [the complaining female student] said Parker made repeated attempts to touch her in a sexually suggestive manner and commented on her breasts. She said he touched her arms, back and legs, and rubbed his arm on her breast. . . . The school district initially suspended Parker for five days without pay but . . . reversed itself after Parker appealed the discipline. . . . A private attorney retained by the school district said the district took appropriate action after the allegations against Parker came to light in 1994. And the allegations of touching, staring and making remarks are comparatively minor, he said. . . . After an investigation in 1994, the district dismissed Parker from his training activities and required him to attend a session on sex and power in the workplace. . . . Parker contested the suspension, and this summer the district dropped it on the condition he withdraw his appeal, acknowledge his participation in sexual harassment classes, and have no further allegations from the date of [the superintendent's] letter until August, 1997. Should that be fulfilled, all evidence of the allegations would be removed from his personnel file but maintained in the district's legal office. . . . The district's investigation revealed a series of complaints by students against Parker and Parker was suspended] . . . for rubbing girls' breasts with his arm as he helped them out with class work; touching, pulling and stroking the hair of a female student; massaging girls' shoulders; and putting his hands on girls' bare legs in class. . . . Parker [allegedly] told one girl the class would "liven up" if she did a table dance and another girl said Parker often made flirtatious comments such as, "You're so beautiful."[3]

The teacher denied all the factual claims by students saying, "The people who know me know I wouldn't do this kind of thing."

There are no allegations of hands under clothing. No overt fondling of breasts or hands on genitals, no penetration, and no intercourse. The allegations do, in fact, present teacher misconduct that is comparatively minor. This is exactly the sort of minor misbehavior that Dr. Rubin believes the school system ought to accommodate by a greater effort at retention. But look what happened here: First, the teacher was not dismissed when the misconduct came to light in 1994, he was given a five-day suspension without pay—and he and his union vehe-

[3]From *The Tacoma News Tribune*, October 25, 1996.

mently objected to even that! Therefore, faced with an arbitration, in the course of which the union would undoubtedly claim that poor Mr. Parker had a "right" to "confront his accusers," meaning all the complaining students would be expected to testify in front of Mr. Parker and open their character and reputation to attack, the school district chose to agree to a record in the personnel file showing that Mr. Parker had erred and had received sex harassment training; the evidence of this to remain in Parker's personnel file for up to three years.

The education association (teacher's union) challenged Parker's short suspension and got it modified to nothing more than having a letter in his personnel file for three years. But notice who got sued here. The school district that agreed with the union got sued; the principal who agreed to the five-day suspension to begin with got sued; and Parker himself got sued. But the union that advocated for retention did not get sued, meaning there is zero reason to think the union will not try to do exactly the same thing again and again, because if the union did not do it for the next miscreant, Mr. Smith for example, then Smith would use the Parker situation to sue the union, claiming it failed to give him (Smith) "fair representation" as compared to what it had earlier done for Parker.

Next, notice that the students sued in 1996 for misconduct, which allegedly occurred between 1991 and 1994 and waited until after they had graduated and were away from Mr. Parker and the school. In Washington, the student has three (3) years after they each reach age eighteen (age of majority) to bring suit.

Finally, there is an aspect of this case that is not apparent from the quote above. It refers to an earlier suit by two girls and their mothers, which had been brought against the same school district based upon alleged sexual harassment by another employee, a hall monitor. This other person was not a teacher and he did not serve in the same building. This other person had no contact with the former students now suing Parker. The only connection (nexus) was that the school district was the same, but the plaintiff's lawyer in the Parker case said about this nexus. "[The Parker lawsuit is] a significant case, because it shows a pattern and practice of the school district failing to take action, not only when it should have known, but when it did know about the inappropriate conduct. . . . It is the exact pattern as Henry—, and girls are being trampled on."

Thus, there is a claim that the school district has exhibited a pattern of indifference to rights of female students. The school district has allegedly done this by repeatedly not being assertive enough in stamping out this misbehavior.

Given these legal concepts, as matters now stand, neither school districts nor individual administrators, such as the principal now being sued in the Parker case, can afford to accept Dr. Rubin's invitation to retain these people and treat them and hopefully cure them. But, just because that is how things are, it does not necessarily follow that is how things should be.

Similarly, as another recent news article points out:

Santa Rosa Case tests harassment ruling

Attorneys this week argued before a federal appeals court that three Santa Rosa educators should not be liable in a Santa Rosa student's $100,000 harassment complaint.

A trial for the former Fremont School student's suit is pending while attorneys on both sides try to settle the issue of whether the girl's former teacher, principal and a Santa Rosa district administrator should be excused from being individually labeled in the case.

The decision has far-reaching implications because if the panel sides with the girl's attorneys, it could mean that educators might have to pay damages in student-to-student sexual harassment cases.

The suit [says] _____ was teased about her body by male classmates and called a lesbian and a slang word for whore. The suit alleges that _____'s former teacher, _____, former principal _____ and _____ director of elementary education, did not take action to stop the alleged harassment.[4]

Here are potential civil claims against individual school officials based upon alleged student-to-student sex harassment rather than teacher-to-student sex harassment. Note the factual basis for this is that a girl was "teased about her body by

[4]From the *Santa Rosa Press Democrat,* October 24, 1996.

male classmates and called a lesbian and a slang word for "whore." That's it. Certainly, most administrators would now opt for retention of the teacher and the principal who were not proactive enough in stopping this alleged misbehavior, but even that traditional response is now being questioned. Can a school district protect itself from these sorts of claims, in the current legal environment, without disciplining teachers and administrators who allow student-to-student sex harassment to continue? Like the situation above involving Mr. Parker, if the Santa Rosa school district had disciplined the teacher and principal who allegedly allowed this harassment to continue, the union would have responded, advocating expungement of the discipline and threatening retaliatory action for injury to business reputation. But, when the lawsuits come, the union does not get sued.

The K–12 legal environment is becoming remarkably like the Mad Hatter's tea party. In my opinion, to do what Dr. Rubin recommends here requires revolutionary thought. First, we have to insist that the union or association which successfully advocates for retention be jointly liable, with management, as to any civil liability claims which result. Next, we must develop a legal mechanism within our court systems that allows a preliminary determination that the retention decision is appropriate—that it is not arbitrary or capricious. Doing this will allow management to retain without exposing the administration and school system to further civil claims. Otherwise, in my opinion, school administrators opting to retain are offering themselves as the next principal in the Tacoma case or in the Santa Rosa case who will be sued for someone else's misconduct.

CHAPTER 5

What to Look for and How to
Avoid Career Destruction

WHAT follows is advice to school personnel intended to fore-warn them of behaviors and situations that can lead to sexual abuse or liaisons between a teacher and student. As you will see, these actions and situations do not constitute crimes but can lead to allegations of criminal activity or to actual crimes. Because a major purpose of this text is to prevent the sexual abuse of students and avoid lawsuits against school systems, we recommend the following list to you.

Some of these ideas are not original and we recognize that the list is not all inclusive. We welcome any additions you wish to contribute. Sadly, we also recognize that even though these suggestions further constrain the staff and may increase the distance between staff and students, we feel that prevention and the avoidance of any suggestion of impropriety is of first importance. We also apologize for any increase in paranoia that educators reading this tome may suffer, but we believe this is the new reality and we all must prepare ourselves to deal with it.

Our suggestions clearly do not apply to the predatory pedo-phile who chooses schools in search of victims. We believe that these persons are a small minority of TSAS but recognize that they do exist and probably always will. Most of the cases we have studied generally concern decent teachers who, because of their present life situation, personality characteristics, the characteristics of the student they are involved with, and the situation they find themselves a part of, get involved in immoral behavior with a student. We believe that through the proactive efforts of school administrators and fellow teachers and parents, the number of these cases can be greatly reduced.

1. Avoid private familial situations. All situations in which teachers are alone with students and unobserved by other adults are risky situations. Only two people can accurately report what happened and they may disagree. Also, a two-person situation can become an intimate or sexualized situation. Closed offices, automobiles, homes, motels, solitary training runs, after-hour workouts, etc., all can become private, risky situations. Make sure there are appropriate chaperones present. Let others know of your meetings. Do not allow staff to interact with students in a closed room or office without another adult present. Do not allow staff to take students home by automobile without another adult being present.

2. Utilize chaperones. Correct chaperoning needs to be spelled out carefully. Away from school and overnight activities pose an area of particular danger. Two or more teachers of the opposite sex or parents or spouses of coaches should be used. The PTA or PTO will usually assist in developing a list of parents willing to chaperone school functions. Anticipate sexual contact between adults and students and develop a plan to avoid it. Make sure everyone involved knows who is in charge and where that person is at all times. When that person is unavailable, make sure everyone knows whom the substitute leader is.

3. When possible, avoid "special relationships." A major concern in psychology relates to why people "click" with each other. Teachers should have a sense for when they begin developing special feelings for a particular student. Fellow staff and administrators should be especially watchful for this circumstance too. The "click" may or may not be reciprocated. It does not have to follow appropriate age or sex or racial guidelines. It is psychological, not logical. For some unknown reason, some people we meet become "sexualized" by us. This may have to do with the attachment and intimacy concepts discussed earlier.

All situations that deviate from the traditional interaction between a teacher and a class or group of students—situations where the teacher–student ratio decreases or the event becomes one-on-one—should be made a focus of special concern and viewed with suspicion. For example, having a teaching assistant, or any sort of personal one-on-one interaction between the staff person and student outside of school.

From Bowlby, Bartholomew, Feeny, Noller, Hazen and Shaver, we see a growing body of research and theory on attachment styles. By educating teachers and administrators we believe we can anticipate these situations and focus on them before any immoral behavior occurs. As humans, we all think and fantasize about each other but we need not act out our fantasies. When that advice is disregarded, however, a fellow staff person or administrator must counsel and forewarn. Then, the staff person at the edge can take appropriate steps to avoid growing closer or being in private situations with the child who is the focus of his or her special attention. These concepts need to be regularly discussed in staff meetings to break down the barriers that inhibit one staff person from reaching out to, or offering to counsel another.

4. Do not socialize with students. Socializing with students, especially off campus or outside school hours is risky business. Teachers and students are people who learn roles and rules. We behave and think in ways that control our role in the educational environment. If we happen to interact with a student in a non-teaching situation, that other "situation" creates a greater likelihood that we will behave unlike a teacher.

Some students and some teachers enjoy non-traditional roles that make their behavior less predictable. There have always been some teachers who pal around with students and enjoy socializing and playing with students. Most do it without intimate involvement. These are valuable teachers who can motivate and work with students in the educational environment, but psychologically some may form relationships with students because of their need for love and acceptance. Most want to be liked. Some have a need to be loved. They feel closer to kids than adults and colleagues and should not socialize with kids. In the most extreme case they may deny their age and position and try to become just "one of the kids." Not a wise choice.

5. *Do not use alcohol or drugs with students.* Use of a disinhibitor, such as alcohol or drugs, in a private situation with a student is a formula for disaster. Many behaviors occur around mind-altering substances that would never occur in situations where these substances were absent. Years ago, in a case that occurred in the state of Washington, two female students acquired a bottle of whiskey and took it to their favorite (bachelor) teacher's home as a present. They insisted he taste it and he did. Shortly thereafter, he concluded that, to show he appreciated the gift, he ought to share it with the two girls, and they then drank the contents of the bottle. Then he suggested that they ought to shower and clean up before he took them home, and they did—together! Then, intoxicated, he drove them to their respective homes and delivered them to their concerned parents. He is no longer a teacher. In another case, a teacher had too much to drink and went to his school's football game where, before hundreds of people, he repeatedly asked a female student to date him. The girl's father, who also happened to be the miscreant's principal, was one of those present. He is no longer a teacher. In another situation, a popular teacher in a small town invited friends and associates to a party at his house. Some high school students showed up and were not turned away. Alcohol and marijuana were in use at the party. He is no longer a teacher.

6. *Avoid gender favoritism or favoritism of particular students.* A teacher or colleague may often notice that another teacher always chooses one student or students of one sex for jobs or positions. Favoritism is not fair, it is dumb. Though the teacher may rationalize that a particular student or group is in need of special attention, the situation will not go unnoticed by other students or other staff. Usually, the students are the first to notice. For example, a teacher who stands behind female students when assisting, but stands beside male students when doing the same thing; a teacher who puts his hands on girls' arms, hair, shoulders, etc., but does not do this with boys; a teacher who eulogizes the boys but not the girls, etc. When favoritism is evident, it should be reported and the offending teacher needs to be required to talk about it to a colleague, preferably a counselor or school psychologist. Dis-

cussing what is occurring with another professional breaks the secrecy and greatly reduces the chance that physical intimacy will develop.

7. Do not give students personal gifts. Giving gifts is generally not a good idea. Always discuss the planned gift with an administrator or colleague before actually giving an item to a student. In the cases studied in this text, for example, a female teacher gave a male student a leather jacket on one occasion and a bike on another. Both male and female teachers have given students pictures or wanted pictures taken with students. Even when the gift-giving is completely aboveboard, it raises unnecessary suspicions in the eyes of other students and staff. There is a pervasive assumption, among both students and adults, that gift-giving lacks legitimate educational purpose.

8. Do not flirt with the students and when the students flirt with adults, exercise best efforts to stop it. While this seems obvious, flirting with students is a common teacher activity. Its roots are probably in the sexual desire of both the teacher and the student. It is often misread by a student who is often too immature to see the social game as fun and superficial. The teacher may delude himself that he is a young stud and desired by the nubile, vestal virgin in his seventh-grade class and worse, he may be! Because the teacher is the adult and is in control, the teacher must work hard to see the situation for what it is, set limits, and control the activities. Puppy love and mad crushes are characteristics of immature students and therefore, this problem must be anticipated and talked about among school staff, all of who should work as a group to protect each other and thus protect the students. Everyone should recognize that intimacy between teachers and students is never good for either group. Sometimes intimacy is beginning and participants cannot see it for what it is. At this point, fellow staff need to be proactive and counsel both the teacher and the student. Puppy love or hero worship between a teacher and student almost always ends badly.

9. Touch a student only when the touch is related to a clear, unmistakably educational purpose. Physical contact between student and teacher is a complex area. A world without physical contact seems cold. Touch is an excellent communication channel and if used wisely can say much that words cannot. But it must be used judiciously and it must be used with the utmost respect for the age and maturity of the student. For example, at the preschool level and early elementary school-age level, students often seek out touching by grabbing the teacher's hand, hugging the teacher, and even kissing the teacher. Often these are children who are not getting enough affection at home. They have a need and they act on it. In general, there is nothing wrong with touching these students, but hugs ought to be from the side rather than the front, the student should not be picked up or cradled in arms, and kissing should not be reciprocated.

Traditionally, in dealing with younger children, K–12 used the "one piece bathing suit" rule, meaning that the torso covered by the suit was off-limits, but that rule is no longer in effect. Now add a hemline at the knee for both boys and girls and avoid the area above that hemline; put sleeves on the one-piece suit extending to the elbow and avoid the area above those sleeves.

Children in the fourth grade up, especially girls between fourth grade and middle school age, are maturing and especially sensitive. When a teacher touches one of these students, he/she should assume the other students, boys and girls, are watching and judging that touch by the values taught at their homes, churches, and at school. Tickling a fourth- or fifth-grade girl under the arms, rubbing a hand along her back at the bra strap level, brushing her hair, putting a hand on her hand, etc., are acts of stupidity that increasingly lead to removal from the teaching profession. In general, with children at these middle grade levels, there should be no roughhousing, wrestling, or horseplay. Hugging and handholding are out, except for a casual hug from the side that, if sought by the student, may be appropriate.

Spanking is allowed in some states. By the fourth-grade level, spanking is questionable. When a child is spanked, however, a wooden instrument should be used to avoid direct touching of the buttocks. The child should be spanked on the buttocks, and that needs to be done by someone who is the same sex as the child and, to avoid demeaning the child, it must be done in a place away from the sight and sound of the other children. None of the child's clothing should be removed. When possible, this scene needs to be played out in the principal's office or another building administrator's office. There should always be another adult witness and a memo reflecting what happened and why for each incident of spanking. An adult who is angry with a student should not be the person doing the spanking or deciding how many whacks the child receives. By the seventh grade spanking is questionable, and by the ninth grade it makes no sense at all.

We recommend children from the seventh or eighth through twelfth grades should not be touched. That includes spanking. The teacher ought to assume everyone is watching and judging. By this age, both the boys and the girls are now biologically mature adults who also happen to be emotionally immature adults. We do not spank them, we do not hit them, and we do not display affection by touching them.

Coaches are particularly exposed to touching complaints. The coach and his or her players are on the bench at the game and it becomes common for the coach to pat a player on the back or buttocks when going into or coming out of the game. Remember, that incident is being watched by the student who is being touched, the other students on the bench, and every spectator in the stands. Coaches are not held to a different standard. What applies in the classroom applies in athletics.

Never touch so much that the student becomes comfortable with the teacher's physical nearness. A teacher, by virtue of position, is not necessarily entitled to access to a student's body. When a teacher is getting sexual satisfaction from touching, that teacher has a problem and needs to be removed from student contact until the problem is corrected. When touching, do not focus solely on what is acceptable to and welcomed by that particular student. Instead, ask what is acceptable to every other student in the educational environment who is exposed to that touching and perhaps in fear that he or she is next.

10. Do not tell off-color stories or allow them to be told in your presence. Be careful about the way you talk to students. Dirty jokes and discussion of sex and bodies may be part of a grooming process, and also may be offensive to someone in the audience. The fourth grade or even tenth grade is not a singles bar. A popular male high school teacher, for example, got into the habit of bantering back and forth with his high school students and sharing off-color stories. He was literally misled by their acceptance. For example, he referred to one girl in his class as "such an airhead she'd be great in a gang bang; she wouldn't know which direction it was coming from." Everyone laughed. Later, when a cheerleader came late to class with a rubberneck brace and a boy asked what happened to —, he replied, "She probably hurt her neck giving head" and almost everyone laughed. The cheerleader didn't. She told her mother, who also didn't laugh. Instead, she went directly to the superintendent and school board president. He lost his job and his teaching certificate.

Remarks about body parts or even attractiveness are now dangerous. Comments such as "You're good looking" or "Nice bod" or "Lookin' good" or "Hey, beautiful" may now be enough to bring a student, her parent(s), and the family lawyer into the teacher's life. But to some students those sorts of comments are not only welcome, they are solicited. For example, a student might comment, "Hey Mr. —, how'm I lookin' today?" or "Do you like what you see?" But one student's welcome is another student's bane because some of the other twenty-five students in the class may well take offense at a casual and welcome comment made to another.

The legal situation has now become even more complex. Now, if a student in the class (rather than the teacher) says the same things and the teacher knew or should have known what was occurring and the teacher fails to take action to prevent recurrence, that teacher is causing or contributing to a hostile educational environment in the form of peer-to-peer sex harassment and can jeopardize his or her teaching position and certificate because of it.

11. Beware of acute emotional crises. Teachers experience emotional turmoil just like everyone else. They go through a death in the family, divorce, child custody disputes, etc., and they get lonely and needy. So do their students. During these periods, unsatisfied emotional needs can lead to poor choices. During these times, a teacher may choose to "help" an emotionally needy student for the wrong reasons. Students may seek teachers out after school, in isolated areas, to "just talk" for the wrong reasons. Staff ought to talk about these situations among themselves and support each other in knowing who among the staff is having trouble and who among the students is, too.

CHAPTER 6

Prevention: A Shared Responsibility

THE cases presented should make all of us realize that teachers that sexually abuse students can be old or young. The TSAS may be a man or a woman, a pedophile or a non-pedophile. The children put at risk may be boys or girls. They may be eight or seventeen. Punishing perpetrators and treating victims will never be our end-all or be-all. Therefore, perhaps we can extract some ideas to prevent, or at least significantly reduce, occurrence.

SECTION I: PREVENTION TECHNIQUES APPLICABLE TO STAFF

This chapter is subtitled "A Shared Responsibility" because we believe that there are several directions we can go with prevention. We will take each of these separately and hopefully provide ideas that you can apply in your educational community. We utilize a pro-active approach, recognizing that TSAS or accusations of TSAS are natural "pitfalls" of the teaching profession. If, as we suggest, TSAS is the product of a variety of factors, then we can expect it to be reduced by the application of a similar variety of solutions.

All school systems, public and private, denominational and nondenominational, are custodians of children. It is the children who draw the attention of the TSAS and therefore, TSAS may occur in any educational system. Consequently, application of the following practices will usually be beneficial in reducing TSAS in any educational system.

Risk Factors—Selection and Hiring

We must be more proactive in our efforts to avoid hiring pedophiles. All persons who apply for employment should be carefully screened. In order to accomplish this, more thorough evaluations should be done. Heightened risk factors should be objectively identified and evaluated. We suggest the following factors ought to cause increased concern:

1. Teachers without a marital history: Pay attention to an applicant who is thirty years of age or older and who has never married. Marriage suggests emotional stability and heterosexual orientation. A history without marriage, however, is not necessarily significant. *Note:* Refusing to consider or interview or hire someone because of marital status or history is marital status discrimination and must be avoided.
2. Teachers with a transient employment pattern: Teachers who move around a great deal are unusual. They may have been asked to move on, or events may have forced them to (see for example, Case 1 in Chapter 3 and the Appendix). When this pattern is present, the prudent thing to do is check with *all* former school employers.
3. Teachers without normal peer relationships: Teachers without friends and social contacts who are age peers are unusual. Similarly, teachers who tend toward social contact with children rather than adults are unusual (see, for example, Cases 3 and 5 in Chapter 3). Most of us tend to enjoy social contacts with people who are approximately our own age. But a teacher who has students who are friends in a positive way may also be the ideal teacher. Be careful not to apply this criterion inappropriately.
4. Teachers with an odd lifestyle: Be especially careful of "odd" people or people who demonstrate bizarre behaviors, such as papering their house windows (see Case 9 in Chapter 3).

Odd does not necessarily mean crazy, and it does not mean sexually dangerous—it just means odd. I can recall explaining this to John Biggs once in this way: "John, some people are crazy, and all of us pretty much agree on who they are. We do not agree on why they are crazy, just that they are. There is another category of people who are not crazy but they are odd. We rarely agree among ourselves on why. One person will say 'weird' and another will say he 'makes me feel uncomfortable' or 'there is something about her I don't like' and usually not understand why they feel that way."

Be careful with this factor. Unusual people tend to be drawn to teaching and their unusual traits are usually their strengths as teachers. All school systems, both public and private, need "odd" people because, without them, the role models some kids need just are not there.

5. Teachers undergoing severe stress: Teachers who are undergoing severe stress caused by domestic disruption as a result of divorce or death in the family are at risk. Teachers who demonstrate symptoms of substance abuse or psychological decompensation are at risk. These sorts of persons can make poor choices and become unintentionally involved with a student.

6. Gregarious and outgoing teachers: Coaches, counselors, music teachers, drama teachers, and art teachers, for example, require more administrative scrutiny than others. This is a group that tends to be a bit unstable (see, for example, Case 8 in Chapter 3). John Biggs noted, for example, that one year he had five teachers on probation, and every one of them was a music teacher who had trouble with classroom management. This is a group that is more likely, in general, to become TSAS.

Psychological Evaluation

In order to avoid hiring a sexual deviant, there are occasions when the human resources or personnel officials of a school district, as a hiring consideration, ought to utilize the services of a clinical psychologist. Preferably, this ought to be a psychologist with training and experience in the diagnosis of deviancy. This option should not, however, be used routinely. Instead, the human resources staff should have some discretion, utilizing risk factors such as those identified above, to pick and choose those persons who should be evaluated. This provision can be written into collective bargaining agreements and into school district policies.

Most school districts have psychologists on staff. These persons are utilized to assess and evaluate students. In particular, they routinely do psychological measurement, assessment, and evaluation by means of psychological and psychoeducational testing. They also identify the seriously behaviorally disabled students who have an inability to build or maintain satisfactory interpersonal relationships and those who engage in inappropriate types of behavior or feelings under normal circumstances. Unfortunately, however, these psychologists are not "clinical psychologists." They do not diagnosis or treat mental, emotional, and behavioral disorders in adults. They also do not provide counseling and guidance by use of psychotherapeutic techniques.

Probationary Behavioral Expectations

School systems ought to have a probationary period during which the new hire's behavioral interactions, particularly with students, are strictly scrutinized. If *any* problems occur, the probationary teacher should be summarily dismissed or be subject to a significant extension of the probationary period. Behavioral restrictions applied during this probation should extend to chaperone duties and practices and address physical interactions with students both at school and away from school. Rules of behavior should be posted in faculty lounge areas and should be strictly enforced.

Currently, this is not routinely done. In Washington State, for example, in-class only observation and evaluation must precede probation. The teacher is rated in the areas of instructional skill, classroom management, professional preparation and scholarship, effort toward improvement when needed, handling of student discipline, interest in teaching pupils, and knowledge of subject matter. No criterion specifically addresses the teacher's behavior when interacting with students, and the teacher's out-of-class behavior is not evaluated at all.

Continuing Education Programs Focusing on Sexual Deviancy

Most school districts do not routinely provide continuing education programs that focus on what is acceptable and what is unacceptable staff interaction with students at school and away from school. This training should be reportedly given to all employees. Staff should be admonished to report unusual or suspicious situations. Programs for staff and faculty that target TSAS prevention will keep this ostrich from sticking its head in the ground. Otherwise, history will repeat itself. In a survey by McIntyre (1987) quoted in Wurtele and Miller-Perrin (1992), only 19% of teachers reported receiving information on this subject during college and only 34% received *any* in-service training on the subject. Presumably, this subject is not being openly discussed with school staff, perhaps because doing so would heighten suspicion within the parent community. We feel that we must focus attention on the obvious need rather than on reasons not to attempt a change. Although it may be worse for staff, it is better for the students if we attack the TSAS problem up front.

Teacher Training Curriculum Should Include Courses on TSAS

Curriculum for teachers should include explanations of normal and abnormal behavior of children at different ages. (One finding is that children who have been or are being abused often demonstrate abnormal sexual activity.) In addition, these curriculums should include instruction on indicators of sexual abuse, the state's mandatory reporting laws, the effects of abuse, and the various theories as to causes of TSAS. For example, Kleemeier et al. (1988) found that a single, comprehensive, six-hour workshop increased teachers' knowledge in all areas and changed their attitudes toward prevention.

In our discussion of theories we often focus on situations. Behavior does not occur in a vacuum and few perpetrators are so disturbed that their abuse occurs in the open classroom or in the lunchroom at noon. Sexual abuse of students usually occurs in private, after hours, off-campus, on trips, in storage rooms, or at the homes of staff or students. The homes of latchkey kids or single-parent homes present opportunities. Teachers and staff must be told in no uncertain terms what situations are no no's. Washington law requires this by declaring, "Except to the extent that he has actual and timely notice of the terms thereof, a person may not in any manner be required to resort to, or be adversely affected by, a matter required to be published or displayed and not so published or displayed" RCW 42.17.250(2).

Every state has a similar requirement. It is a basic concept of jurisprudence: We announce what is expected, we enforce that standard, and we punish those who do not comply. Years ago, new teachers were often given a "mop talk" by an older and ostensibly wiser colleague. The new teacher was told where and how they could and could not touch students. While this was an old-fashioned practice, perhaps we should not have swept it away so quickly. Such a demonstration may get the message out to teachers and staff and be useful in establishing the current teacher–student relationship.

Chaperones must be provided from either staff or parents. We must let parents know that if an activity is important enough for their child, they must sacrifice their time and energy for that activity. If they say, "I am too busy" or "It is the teacher's job," they are denying their shared responsibility and need to be told that. Teachers are not paid to deal with children after hours, on weekends, on trips, or at home. If they are willing to spend extra time and energy so should parents. Remember, because chaperones can be dangerous, be sure you know who the chaperone is. Beginning employees (and volunteers) require an especially close watch. Until trust is earned, never trust anyone. At some level, whenever a teacher or staff person is alone with a student, it is a dangerous situation, but when two or more adults are present, it is highly unlikely that abuse will occur.

Proactively Avoid Indifference

One of the most damaging accusations found in most TSAS civil suits is a claim that the educational atmosphere within the school system permitted abuse, or previous cases had received either minimal investigation or minor punishments. No school system or school administrator wants the following publicity:

> Ex-student says principal was told about abuses.
>
> Davenport High School Principal Harold _____ was warned in 1991 that a guidance counselor now facing federal charges was enticing girls to model lingerie, a former student says.
>
> "I got real mad when Mr. _____ told the students last week that we should have gotten off our butts and come to him with this stuff because I did just that" said Josie _____, now 19.
>
> "Another student's parents said they went to _____ in February, 1991 with concerns about Jungblom.
>
> "School Board's Silence Shouts 'Failure' . . . See no evil. Speak no evil. Hear no evil." That should have been the caption underneath Friday's picture in the *Spokesman-Review*, which showed three members of the Davenport School Board.[5]

> Grand Jury Indicts School Counselor . . .
> Porn Ring Investigation Includes Others
>
> . . . Girls involved in the case said they initially were enticed to model lingerie, then promised more money for partial nudity. The biggest payment went to girls who agreed to film pornography, including group sex. . . .
>
> . . . A former student said she wanted to attend college after graduating from Davenport High School in June, 1991 but her family didn't have the money. . . . When she went to see Jungblom [the Counselor] about her transcript and scholarship possibilities "he told me I could make more money working on my back.[6]

In serious cases there is often a pattern of repetitive behavior

[5]From *Spokesman-Review,* January 25, 1994.
[6]From *Spokesman-Review,* February 7, 1994.

(see, for example Case 6 in Chapter 3). Once the situation becomes apparent, the entire pattern begins to unfold. Often the pattern has been forming for several years. Do not focus only on the current event or the current school year. Always ask, what is the history? If you don't ask the question and answer it, someone else will.

Offer Open-Door Counseling to Staff

There should be a resource person who the faculty and staff can go to if fantasies and feelings about students arise. This might lead to an ongoing, confidential group where feelings are discussed and acknowledged. If we can accept the fact that sexual feelings for students are a natural part of the teaching profession, a proactive approach allows teachers to discuss these feelings and develop preventative strategies to avoid physical contact. In relapse prevention programs with sex offenders, we discuss feelings, precautions, and avoidance procedures.

However, we wish to emphasize that what is suggested here is an open door to discuss *thoughts and feelings,* not actual grooming or touching. Once the latter occurs, every state requires that the abuse be reported. See Washington, RCW 26.44.030, requiring report within forty-eight clock hours of knowledge being received. These laws are personal—meaning that whomever receives the information has a duty to report.

SECTION II: PREVENTION TECHNIQUES APPLICABLE TO STUDENTS

A second area of prevention is a child-focused program. In all cases of TSAS there are children. Some of these are preschoolers who are totally naive about sexuality, and some are high school seniors with extensive sexual histories. We feel that reducing the incidence of TSAS requires that we understand the characteristics of the victims. Schools and parents can educate children to make them less vulnerable. Programs can be general in nature or target specific groups. For instance, techniques and curriculums have been developed that focus on developmentally disabled children. These kids, who are a high at-risk group, but can be educated to become more resistant and hence less likely to be victimized.

There are several objectives of child-focused programs, and it is easy to see that children of different ages will require different content and different teaching techniques. While some parents may object to a "sex education program," we believe that few parents will object to safety programs. Safety programs for younger students emphasize a "touch continuum" (Anderson, 1979) and "private parts" rather than explicitly correct sexual terms. Young children are made aware of their rights concerning their bodies and their right to object to people who invade their body zone. Communication is stressed, such as the need to tell parents rather than keeping secrets. While the term *empowerment* is used with older children, the same concept can be discussed with little tykes. Parents, as well as professionals, can teach kids that certain situations are dangerous and must be avoided.

Wurtele and Miller-Perrin (1992) have done an excellent job of summarizing the effectiveness of child-focused programs. They found that programs using more active modes of training were generally more effective than purely didactic approaches. This should make us all aware that doing a program does not mean that children have learned anything. Further, even if they "learned" something, it does not necessarily translate into reduced incidents of TSAS.

They are critical of studies that attempt to show effectiveness of programs. In their survey of research on effectiveness they concluded that many variables, including intelligence, abuse status, community values, home background, parents' attitudes about prevention, etc., influence the impact of such a program on the children receiving it. We have reached a point when we can say that some child-focused programs will prove effective with some children as measured by some measurers. Superficial, general dictums and a "one-program fits all" approach have proven to be archaic and untrue.

One area that seems to be little researched is the adolescent program. As we consider the pubescent and postpubescent student, special issues arise. For instance, this is probably the most abused group and attracts the greatest number of potential perpetrators. As society has lowered the age for sexually intimate behavior, we run a risk of tacitly approving our children's sexual activities. We allow these children greater freedom of movement and even respect their privacy and secrets. As they push to become adults they play right into the hands of teachers anxious to get their hands on them in inappropriate ways. Many famous people publicly flaunt sexual relationships with much younger partners. Does this encourage teachers to do the same? Does our honoring this subtly alter the standards of acceptability to society as a whole? As suggested in *The Hurried Child* (Elkind, 1981), are parents pushing children to grow up early? If we value the youthfulness of certain teachers, such as coaches, and value the preciousness of teenage students, are we constructing the bed where they will meet? Do they perceive themselves as having our blessing? Clearly, we need programs focusing on "amorous" interactions between pubescent students and their teachers. By analogy, date rape programs focus on both victims and perpetrators. Perhaps we need similar teacher–student programs for both populations. *A word of caution:* We need to carefully consider the negative effects of child-focused prevention programs. Again, Wurtele and Miller-Perrin (1992) do a great service in summarizing the research. They find no evidence of short- or long-term negative effects from such programs. They end their review of child sexual abuse prevention programs by highlighting four underlying themes: remember, recognize, resist, and report, and urge programs to promote healthy sexuality that is age appropriate, rather than merely focusing on the dangers of abuse.

SECTION III: PREVENTION TECHNIQUES FOR PARENTS

This section is intended to assist parents in learning how to prevent TSAS and how to respond when it occurs.

Parents have the primary responsibility for raising children. They are legally responsible for them from birth to adulthood and may even be liable for their juvenile children's misbehaviors. It seems that in our complicated society many of us attempt to casually pass this responsibility off to babysitters, preschools, and educational institutions. Even at the college level we hear whispers of *in loco parentis* (in place of the parent). Parents often seem anxious to blame whoever was supposedly caring for their children. However, parents remain responsible, and, more importantly, if unhappy events occur, it is the parents as well as the child who must endure the consequences. Shared responsibility means that both parents and the school system must accept responsibility for raising a child. The school system is limited by what it can and cannot do. In part, this is due to the public's financial support for the school system, or lack of it.

Finklehor (1984) and Porch and Petretic-Jackson (1986) found that parents are less likely to discuss sexual abuse with young children than other topics such as death or kidnapping. "Stranger-Danger" is more often discussed than general safety rules or sexual abuse (Berrick, 1988, and Gilbert, 1988). In fact, some researchers believe that emphasis on child sexual abuse moved from intrafamily to extrafamily perpetrators during the early 20th century (Wurtele and Miller-Perrin, 1992). Eventual research, however, has confirmed that known individuals, not strangers, perpetrate most sexual abuse. Recently, there appears to be a greater interest by parents in child sexual abuse programs. Several recent surveys quoted in Wurtele and Miller-Perrin's book, *Preventing Child Sexual Abuse,* demonstrate that parents want to know about preventative programs at school and generally support these types of programs. While such programs vary, the major objectives, according to Wurtele and Miller-Perrin, are informing parents about the problem, educating parents on how to teach their children about sex abuse prevention, assisting parents in identifying sexual abuse victims, and teaching parents appropriate responses to disclosures by child victims.

Parents of victims generally tend to be angry at the school system. In part, this can to be a form of denial that allows them to avoid facing their own failures. Their explosive and unrealistic anger is often not rational. Perhaps at an unconscious level, they realize that they could have taken better care of their sons and daughters. Instead of having to face the truth that their own laziness or lack of priorities was partly responsible for the abuse of their children, parents would often rather attack the school system.

Accept a Share of Responsibility for our Children's Education

Parents should accept some responsibility for reduction of TSAS events. The following suggestions are intended to assist parents in achieving that goal:

1. *Teacher hiring:* Parents should seek to participate in the hiring or tenuring process. This can be done through committee appointments or parent–teacher organizations.
2. *Know the teacher:* When children are involved in extraordinary activities there is increased risk of TSAS. Insist on knowing the teacher who is supervising a child's play, his or her athletic teams, or off-campus trips.
3. *Communication with children:* Keep the lines of communication open, so your children feel free enough to discuss serious relationships and concerns about teachers. Successful abusers often focus on children who are not likely to discuss such concerns with parents.
4. *Family sex education:* Educate your children about sex and relationships between the sexes. Falling in love with teachers and teachers flirting with students are not uncommon. These situations can and should be discussed.
5. *Participate in child's education:* Be more willing to act as a chaperone or volunteer to sit in an auditorium during a late night rehearsal. Parents can help school officials write clear chaperone guidelines that ensure adequate coverage and supervision outside normal classroom situations. Always know who is chaperoning your children, and when you do not trust them, say so.

What Parents Should Do When Abuse Occurs

When parents learn of alleged sexual improprieties between

a child and a school official, the following guidelines may assist in dealing more effectively with the situation at hand:

1. *Listen, believe, and support:* Talk to your son or daughter and believe them. Generally, supporting the victim helps to reduce the trauma. Remember, though, that kids do lie, and allegations might not be true. Kids will often disclose what occurred in stages. Do not discourage them from adding to the disclosure as time goes by. Some research suggests that 40–50% of child sex abuse allegations fail to be substantiated. *But, that does not mean something inappropriate did not occur.*

2. *Do not panic:* The child is relying upon your strength and wisdom. It is not the end of the world. Even children who are victims of abuse can grow up to be healthy, happy, productive members of the community. It is partly the parents' response, at the time, that is crucial to successful recovery. Life offers us many misfortunes and parents can help teach and model healthy responses to negative events.

3. *Do not overgeneralize:* Statements such as "all men are like that" or "all teachers do that" or "sex is disgusting" do not help the victim deal with what has happened.

4. *Help children to learn from their mistakes:* Help your child understand what part he or she played in the abuse. This assists them in taking hold of their life and becoming more responsible for their future. Even victims of rape usually make some poor choices, such as allowing themselves to be alone in a place and time where the abuser could take advantage. They are ultimately the pilots of their own existence. At an early age, children can begin accepting some of the responsibility. This does not mean they caused their own abuse. It means they had and will have much to say about their own lives. Remember, "we are all victims."

5. *Work with not against the school system:* Try not to just blame. When the school system takes action against the teacher, offer support as a witness. Help find other witnesses. Do what you can to protect future children from abuse. Help reshape that system to minimize future risk.

Minimizing the Victim's Trauma

From a practical point of view, parents and school officials need to understand that events alone do not cause psychological trauma. From what we know about human psychology, it is how we process information rather than the information itself that affects us psychologically. A group of people experiencing the same event, e.g., an airplane crash or auto accident, will have different sequa (psychological scars). Each of us sees the world and ourselves differently. A cognitive-behavioral model of human psychology suggests that how we interpret events and how we view ourselves influence how traumatic an event will be.

The most common counseling process for victims of traumatic sexual events is for the counselor or therapist to help the victim see themself as an innocent victim, not as someone responsible for the molestation or rape. This allows the victim to be angry with the perpetrator instead of themselves. A period of "catharsis" seems appropriate, and often includes anger, sorrow, self-pity, asking for support, depression, and regression. After this process, most counselors will assist the victim to regain strength and self-assertion. Eventually, depending somewhat on age, the victim must begin to accept responsibility for his or her own life. From Abraham Maslow to Carl Rogers to Albert Bandura, we see the general proposition that psychologically healthy people take responsibility for their own lives and seek to actualize their potential. Thus, wallowing in the "victim stance" is hardly the endpoint of successful psychotherapy.

The psychological effects of being abused by a teacher are variable and we believe they can be minimized. First, the adults whom the child confides in must support and acknowledge the child. The trusted teacher's misbehavior represents a tear in the security blanket surrounding the child; this adult who was loved and admired and supposedly protective has shattered the cozy womb of healthy development. From the moment that the child reveals the abuse, we must reaffirm to the child that the world is made up of supportive, protective, and trustworthy adults. The abusive teacher was the exception, not the rule. The child is still loved and respected, and the world is still a good place to be.

The child's sense of shame, guilt, and dirtiness will usually have existed for some time. We need to start reversing the processes that led to those feelings. Aphrodite Matsakis (1992), an expert on trauma recovery, points out that the victim has lost both the sense of invulnerability in an ordinary world and the positive view of self. We need to immediately say, both with actions and words, you are a good person, we care for and trust you, and what happened was not your fault. Ideally, our optimism is infectious. We need to let the child know that things will work out and that past events do not mean that the future will be terrible. Parents and counselors often make a mistake in treatment by leaving a child to feel that the molestation was horrible and that he or she will remain disturbed for many years or perhaps forever. In that regard, Anna Freud studied English children who were in London during World War II when the Germans bombed the city. She found that each child's degree of fear and trauma was not related to the severity of the bombing, but to the reactions of the adults with the children during and afterwards. Similarly, having one's crotch touched or having an adult expose himself to a child is an event that awaits psychological interpretation. Counselors, parents, and even attorneys can affect how the child thereafter sees him or herself and the event itself. If we terribilize it, we exacerbate the child's negative reaction. Put another way, what is more important—winning a large financial settlement or helping a child to quickly regain mental and emotional health? For example, in the McMartin Preschool case in Southern California, the legal disputes wound on for seven years. Repeated interviews, newspaper accounts, and participation in television shows did not help the children to recover. Instead, it probably increased the trauma.

A case in John Biggs's experience illustrates these points. The situation occurred in a fifth-grade classroom and involved the abuse of several girls. The male teacher was a reader in the local Catholic church and a scoutmaster. To most of the victims, he was their first male teacher. One day Carie went home and began crying uncontrollably. Her mother asked her why and she claimed she had a stomachache. Her mother believed her and sent her to bed. Carie cried through the night, and as the hours sped by, her mother was there beside her. Carie then described how the teacher, Mr. Smith, would insist that girls needing help come up front to his desk and stand beside him while he sat at the desk facing the class. When Carie did this, Mr. Smith would put his arm around her waist. Lately, he had begun rubbing his arm against her upper thigh and buttocks. Her mother believed her, supported her, and was not critical. But Carie was not done. When it was apparent to Carie that her Mom was not going to be angry, she described how Mr. Smith had asked her to stay after school and then asked her to go down into the basement storeroom and get a box for him. She described how scared she was. Then, she described how Mr. Smith had come into the storeroom behind her and hugged her and how afraid she was. Her mother stayed with her throughout the night, the next day, and during the interviews by school officials and lawyers. But Carie was not done: A few days later she described how Mr. Smith had then taken down his pants and put her hands on his penis. A few days later, she described how he had asked her to kiss it and how she had kissed it. Carie felt dirty. She was ashamed and scared and uncertain of everyone and everything. Once Carie told her story though, investigation revealed five more girls in the same class who had been fondled or abused by Mr. Smith. None had told their parents.

Besides accepting the victim's accounts and supporting them emotionally, the adult's demeanor and optimism is critical. The legal procedures that follow disclosure should be as efficient as possible. A single videotaped interview between a supportive parent and a trained interviewer who has been previously introduced to the victim seems to be the best course to follow. Ideally, in previous sessions the interviewer will have made friends with the victim and hopefully shown the victim that he or she is trustworthy and supportive.

Multiple interviews and cross-examinations of a child by attorneys and police can, but need not, exacerbate the trauma. Jan Hindman, who is a sensitive expert child interviewer, points out that children are often traumatized by the investigation and that "years of therapeutic intervention are added to the original problem of exploitation" (Hindman, 1987, p. 5).

She advises that victim interviewing must be adjusted to the developmental age of the victim. We must focus on both prosecutorial needs for a good interview and recuperative process.

In Carie's case however, there were multiple interviews by lawyers and by police, and eventually she testified against Mr. Smith. At age eleven, Carie sat in a closed school hearing with her mother at her side, faced Mr. Smith across the table, and testified in detail about what he had done to her. Mr. Smith was dismissed; he lost his teaching certificate and never taught again. Two years later, Mr. Smith was caught abusing his stepdaughter and was sent to prison. Along the way, Carie was society's most important person. She undoubtedly protected future female students from abuse by Mr. Smith and she knew it. Carie is an emotionally healthy woman now. To Carie, going through the process was therapy.

The foregoing points out an endemic problem in dealing with TSAS in K–12 public education. This is the negotiation of *contractual* due process procedures incorporated into collective bargaining agreements between teacher associations and school districts. These procedures often effectively prevent our judicial system from protecting a child witness. Instead, the teacher may be allowed to attack the victim. In Mr. Biggs's experience, this has happened repeatedly: Teachers insist upon the "right to confront an accuser" and then insist that the "accuser," even if only eleven or twelve years of age, testify alone and in person. The teacher's real hope is that the child will be intimidated by the process and not testify at all, the teacher then asks for dismissal of the charge for lack of evidence. This is a grievance–arbitration process that allows no judicial intervention. This process is not victim oriented. It is not a process that was ever agreed to by parents or child victims, and it has to be changed. The process itself is a form of child abuse that serves no useful public purpose. Laws must be changed to protect the victims by allowing use of videotape testimony and avoiding confrontation of the accuser in teacher dismissal cases involving sexual abuse.

Seeing a therapist for years is not necessarily a good way for a child to spend his or her life. Therapeutic contact represents an ongoing unusual event in the life of a child. It says to the child, "You are different and you are damaged." Perhaps for some children, we should say "No, you are like all children and you are OK." In some cases, it appears that counselor–therapist interactions are actually harmful in the sense that the healing process is unnecessarily prolonged. Psychotherapy has not reached the point where we can say to a victim, "Take two years of therapy and call me in the morning." Estimates of future therapy needs, which are given in civil trials as proof of future economic damages, are, at best, questionable. Generally, we cannot predict with accuracy the future therapy needs of the individual victim.

The child-victim should be carefully watched for any indication that the abuse is causing emotional problems. Some common indicators are regressions such as bedwetting, baby talk, sleep disorders, eating problems, self-abusing behaviors, mood disturbance, academic difficulties where none previously existed, self-blame, perfectionism, age inappropriate behaviors, and anger. Matsakis (1992) goes on to discuss many potential behavioral reactions. However, we emphasize that therapists only see the victims who are not coping well. There are those, such as Carie, who therapists never see and who seem to handle the molestation well. However, there is also another group. They have less obvious symptoms such as withdrawal, daydreaming, and chosen social isolation. They may choose those courses rather than choosing disclosure.

Professionals and parents should meet regularly to discuss victims' progress. In some cases therapeutic intervention will be required to assist the child in developing a healthy self-concept, a healthy view of his or her sexuality, and a healthy view of the world.

CHAPTER 7

Negligent Hiring and Negligent Retention

OVERVIEW

THERE is little a K–12 administrator can do that will end a career faster than either hiring or (worse) retaining a sexual molester who hurts kids. It is almost impossible to explain retention. Society has adopted a "no tolerance" policy. Judges may listen to excuses, but juries generally do not.

Within the subsets of "negligent hiring" and "negligent retention" the degree of potential damage is a significant determinant: It is more excusable to hire someone who purloins tools or steals money than it is to hire or retain someone who abuses children. Perhaps in an ideal world, courts would react to each of those hypothetical cases in the same way, but this is not an ideal world.

NEGLIGENT HIRING

This is clearly an emerging concept. In its simplest terms, it means that when hiring, there is a duty to that class of persons exposed to risk (e.g., students) to investigate the applicant accordingly. When injury occurs, the claim is made that,

1. There was a duty to investigate more thoroughly than was actually done.
2. If the investigation had been conducted at the proper level of intensity, the school district would have learned that the

prospective employee had earlier engaged in conduct suggesting foreseeable future risk.

3. Because of that foreseeable risk, a reasonable employer, knowing the prospective employee's true history, would not have entrusted students to his or her care.

4. There is a causal connection between the decision to hire or the decision to retain the employee and the injury to the victim, meaning reoccurrence of the sort of misconduct engaged in at an earlier time will expose an identifiable class of persons to foreseeable risk.

5. Since the school district "should have known" the employee's true history, it is liable for injury to the student who suffered injury at the hands of the employee.

While imposition of liability for negligent hiring is relatively new, imposing liability on account of negligent retention is not. Even so, both concepts are now routinely treated as legally synonymous, e.g., "We can ascertain no substantial difference in imposing a duty on an employer to use reasonable care in the initial hiring from his duty to use that care in the retention of an employee."[7]

NEGLIGENT RETENTION

A negligent retention case generally has its genesis in suspicions that arise at work or in private life that are work related. For example, if an employee is investigated for allegedly sexually abusing his stepdaughter, the allegation relates to a child of student age. Even though the alleged abuse is not claimed to have occurred at school, a prudent K–12 administrator hearing a rumor of this sort of misconduct ought to pursue it and check further. The degree of alleged risk and foreseeability of *possible* risk must be considered when deciding whether or not to pursue the information. Correspondingly, the source of the rumor or suspicion usually ought not govern pursuit. For example, an anonymous phone call or letter suggesting an

[7]*Ponticas v. K.M.S. Investments,* 331 N.W. 2d 907, 911 (Minn. 1983), citing to Restatement (Second) Agency, Sec. 213.

employee is prone to sexually abuse is worthy of further investigation unless the source of the information is known and known to be unreliable. An anonymous source is not known to be unreliable and therefore the information ought to be pursued. When in doubt, ask your school attorney.

For example, several years ago a private secondary school academy administrator called describing how a faculty member, who had served as a missionary faculty member in a Third-World boarding school, had returned to the United States with one of his students, an eleven-year-old girl. Since then, fellow faculty, neighbors, and even the man's wife had questioned his familial relationship with this young girl. Noting that none of this had occurred at school and there had been no "work-related" rumors, the administrator wanted to know if the administration had any duty to pursue (investigate) the faculty member's relationship with the girl. It was obvious the caller wanted the answer to be "no" and it should be obvious to the reader that the answer is "yes." The vignette presents concerns about a familial relationship with a female of student age. Assuming the concerns are valid and the faculty member's relationship with the child is sexually exploitive, there is foreseeable risk to a clearly identifiable class of persons—females of student age. Even though the information relates to the faculty member's "private life" it must be pursued.

Negligent retention cases are anathema to human resources staff. When an employee has done something or failed to do something that *may* suggest future risk staff often disagrees about foreseeability of risk. The school district usually has a "progressive discipline" policy requiring that the least form of discipline be applied to remediate. "Employee rights," often codified in a "collective bargaining agreement," an employee handbook, school district policy, or all of the above, begin to impact the health, safety, and welfare of the students—and neither the students nor their parents approved that collective bargaining agreement. The human resources staff is forced to balance risk to students against employment rights of the accused, while the union or association is insisting on retention. Later, though, the retained employee may hurt kids. When injury to a *future* student occurs, the employing school district, and, perhaps, the administrators making the retention decision are liable and the union is not. It makes no difference that the employee is a teacher, librarian, custodian, bus driver, or anyone else invested with student conduct by virtue of their employment.

Often, human resource staff must choose who to be sued by, the employee and union or association for "wrongful discharge" or the potential victim of sexual abuse for "negligent retention." In some cases, management will support a discharge knowing that the union will take the matter on to arbitration or appeal, and knowing that, as a probability, the discharge will be overturned. This is inexpensive insurance against a future "negligent retention" case by a *future* student who may be injured as a result of the employee's retention.

KNEW OR SHOULD HAVE KNOWN STANDARD

Historically, there was apparently some merit in denying the obvious, and consequently, many K–12 administrators denied having seen or heard any evil. Society responded with application of the "knew or should have known" standard. As a result, no court today gives must credence to a K–12 administrator's denials. Now, the question is whether a *reasonable administrator* should have known, that is, a *reasonable administrator* from the same state, not the same town. When the issue focuses on sexual abuse of children, the answer is almost always "yes." Today, the "see no evil, hear no evil" rationalization is really nothing more than a career-ending experience for many K–12 administrators.

Imposition of liability for negligent retention is sometimes confused with the *respondeat superior* concept wherein liability for actions or inactions of an employee (a servant) is imposed vicariously on the employing school district (because of the relationship). As a general rule, "vicarious" liability *is not imposed* as a consequence of "negligent retention."[8] Instead, a different legal concept altogether is applied:

[8]*Bratton v. Calkins,* 73 Wn. App. 492, 501, 870 P. 2d 981 (1994).

There must be some causal relationship between the dangerous propensity or quality of the employee, of which the employer has or should have knowledge, and the injuries suffered by the third person; the employer must, by virtue of knowledge of his employee's particular quality or propensity, have reason to believe that an undue risk of harm exists to others as a result of the continued employment of that employee; and the harm which results must be within the risk created by the known propensity for the employer to be liable.[9]

For example, in a recent case, the parents claimed that a school bus driver had sexually molested a small child.[10] Physical evidence supported the contention that the child had been repeatedly sexually abused. In separate interviews with separate interviewers the child made consistent reports, claiming that the abuse occurred on the school bus while sitting in the driver's lap or beside the driver. There was corroborating evidence proving that the driver routinely had small children sit on his lap. Also, there was evidence proving that at times the bus was inexplicably stopped along the side of the road between bus stops. Altogether, even though the driver denied molesting this child in particular, or any child, there was sufficient evidence to prove molestation occurred.

The driver (Lamson) had no criminal background and no history of psychological problems. When he was hired, he had a valid school bus driver's permit. That meant that he had a valid driver's license, he had passed a physical examination checking both physical and mental health, he had completed a first aid course and a driving safety course, and he had no convictions for a variety of serious crimes including sex crimes and assaults. Prior to hire, Mr. Lamson had completed four years as a special education bus driver for another school district. This previous employer had terminated Lamson for "lateness and tardiness" explaining that he had a second job and he enjoyed stopping and speaking to parents and children.

[9]*Kansas State Bank v. Specialized Tr. Serv.*, 819 P. 2d 587, 596 (1991), quoting from *Hollinger v. Stormont Hosp. & Training School for Nurses,* 2 Kan. App. 2d 302 at 307, 578 P. 2d 1121 (1978).

[10]*Giraldi v. Community Consolidated School District,* 279 Ill. App. 3d 679, 665 N.E. 2nd 332 (1996).

As a result, he tended to be chronically late, and for that reason he was let go.

With the current school employer (District 62), there had been three complaints about Lamson during the school year, all pertaining to him being late along his bus route. There was evidence that another mother (Levin) had been concerned enough about the lateness and possible stopping en route that she "tailed" the bus. But she also testified that she had never considered that Lamson's dilatory driving meant that sexual abuse of the students was taking place.

In this case, the jury was allowed to hear evidence of negligent hire, in particular, the evidence that Lamson had been let go by the previous employer, Davidsmeyer, as a result of "chronic lateness and tardiness." The jury also heard evidence of negligent retention, in particular, evidence that there had been three complaints against Lamson at Community Consolidated School District Number 62 due to lateness. But the evidence indicated that foreseeable risk to the victim (the student) was not within the known risk (likelihood that Lamson would be tardy), e.g.,

> The only thing Septran [a private bus company that was the current employer, contracted to provide bus service to the school district] could have known was that Lamson had a tendency to be late. There is no factual or logical relationship between that knowledge and the attack on Daniel. Even if Septran was negligent in hiring a driver who had trouble being on time, that does not establish a proximate cause relationship to the injury to Daniel.[11]
>
> A cause of action for negligent hiring is proved by evidence that the employer knew or reasonably should have known the person who was hired was unfit for the job in the sense that the employment would place the employee in a position *where his unfitness* would create foreseeable danger to others. . . . It must be a "particular unfitness" which creates a danger of harm to others. . . . In addition, any negligence in hiring or retaining the employee must be the proximate cause of the plaintiff's injuries.[12]

[11]Ibid. pg. 340.
[12]Ibid. pg. 339.

Lamson's history raised reasonable suspicion of foreseeable risk that he could be chronically tardy. In fact, he was tardy at his previous employer, Davidsmeyer, and he was tardy at the current employer, District 62. But his history suggested no foreseeable risk that he would sexually abuse students. Nonetheless, he apparently did just that. Therefore, Lampson was liable but the current employer, District 62, was not.

However, if Davidsmeyer had concerns about sexual abuse and failed to document them and failed to rely upon them as a basis for the termination decision, then Davidsmeyer arguably engaged in a misrepresentation by silence to District No. 62, and consequently failed its duty to a clearly identifiable class of persons who would be exposed to foreseeable risk if Lamson were allowed to continue in student contact—that classification or category comprised of persons of student age.

All schools and school administrators owe a duty of care to *all* children.[13] Therefore, negligent retention can be applied, even if the miscreant employee has left your school district and moved on to another. This is a form of *negligent entrustment,* which applies to *"one who supplies directly or through a third person"* In the school setting, this can mean that when the hiring was caused or contributed to by the failure of a previous employer (e.g., Davidsmeyer) to fully disclose problems to the prospective employer (e.g., District 62) and when the abuser, often years later, hurts a student at District 62, and the student and/or parents sue District 62 claiming negligent hiring or negligent retention, District 62 will have a claim against Davidsmeyer. The claimant must prove that the employee who caused or contributed to the plaintiff's injury was unfit for hiring, that the employment of this person was a proximate cause of the plaintiff's injury, and that the employer either knew or should have known of the employee's lack of fitness.[14] When there is any question whatsoever about a prospective new hire, consult your school attorney.

It is *possible* to avoid a successful negligent hiring case when there is reliance upon either overt misrepresentation or mis-

[13]Ibid. fn. 3, pg. 596, quote from *Hollinger.*
[14]Ibid. fn. 1.

representation by silence and no other factual basis to conduct an extraordinary investigation (to look further). But, when the injury is sexual abuse to a student, claimants are often allowed to argue to a jury that there was some factual basis to look further, and a look further would have avoided injury to the claimant. For example, millions of dollars in damages were awarded to a woman who had been forcibly raped by her cabdriver. Prior to the rape, the Fort Worth Cab and Baggage Company had accepted the rapist, Jenkins, as a cabdriver because he had a taxi driver's license.[15] The police department indicated that it would have informed the cab company if "an applicant had any convictions on his record." In retrospect, that seems unlikely. Jenkins had been arrested for theft and convicted for forgery. He had been convicted twice for robbery and once for theft. Then he had been indicted for attempted murder of a woman with a hammer and was pending trial at the time he began his employment with Fort Worth Cab & Baggage.

In another case,[16] a resident apartment manager violently sexually assaulted one of the female tenants. The rapist, Graffice, had been employed as apartment manager, incident to which, he was issued a passkey that allowed him access to all the residential units. Thereafter, he raped a tenant at knifepoint. Prior to getting this position, Graffice had been in the Army and was given a general discharge (suggesting unfitness). Thereafter, he was charged with burglary and possession of stolen property, convicted and sentenced to several months in jail. Thereafter, he moved to another state and was charged with burglary, theft, and armed robbery. He was convicted of burglary and armed robbery and spent time in prison. Thereafter, he obtained employment as a driver for the "Spring Lake Park School Bus Company." Fortunately for the students in his charge, Graffice drank on the job, argued with his boss, and was fired.

When Graffice sought employment as an apartment manager, he was asked to fill out a standard form. He was asked for the names of two references. He provided one without any

[15]*Salinas v. Fort Worth Cab & Baggage Co., Inc.,* 725 S.W. 2d 701, 703 (1987).
[16]Ibid. fn.1.

address and provided no phone numbers for either. The references were not pursued, which may have been just as well since the references turned out to be Graffice's mother and sister. Initially, Graffice did not get the job; instead, the job was offered to another party, who surprisingly turned it down. Then, needing someone right away, Graffice was interviewed. He was asked about convictions and indicated he had "traffic tickets." His explanation was not pursued. In fact, at the time he applied for the apartment manager position, Graffice was on supervised parole. He was hired without further investigation. Later, the hiring official testified that she would not have hired Graffice if she had known of his criminal record, and Graffice testified that, if he had been asked to sign a release of criminal records, he would have withdrawn his application.

The Court defined the applicable legal standard in the following way: "Liability is predicated on the negligence of an employer in placing a person with known propensities, or propensities which should have been discovered by reasonable investigation, in an employment position in which, because of the circumstances of the employment, it should have been foreseeable that the hired individual posed a threat of injury to others."

Imposition of liability was upheld. In the process, the Court rightly concluded that there is no *absolute* duty to check for a criminal record: "Liability of an employer is not to be predicated solely on failure to investigate criminal history of an applicant but, rather, in the totality of the circumstances surrounding the hiring, whether the employer exercised reasonable care. . . . Here, the jury could have found . . . slight effort to determine whether it was safe to hire Graffice."

In the K–12 setting, the "totality of the circumstances" includes consideration of the age and maturity of the students who will be exposed to the employee. Also, both the potential and actual degree of adversity to the students must be considered, and sexual abuse is the most serious form of adversity, meaning extraordinary investigation is appropriate to the new hire, and consideration of foreseeable risk attendant to retention must be considered.

For example, several years ago a band teacher in an eastern

Washington school district was hired and subsequently abused a male high school student. This fellow had come from another Washington school district where he had taught successfully for a year. There was no indication in this previous employment suggesting he was prone to abuse.

The teacher had a Washington State teaching certificate. To get it, he had successfully undergone a Washington State Patrol records check, which is a check of *Washington only* criminal records. He was asked if he had been convicted of any crime in the past seven years, answered "no," and was hired. In fact, he had been convicted twice in California for consensual sodomy in a public place. A thorough investigation in California would have uncovered these earlier convictions. If the convictions had been known, he would not have been hired, but his hiring was not negligent.

Increasingly, negligent retention has become an issue when dealing with any employee who has been complained against for sexual harassment. In a recent case, the claimant presented civil sexual harassment allegations in the form of negligent hiring and negligent retention claims.

The Court concluded that this was done solely to extend liability to the employer and dismissed the claims, indicating that the claimant ought to pursue administrative claims first through the State Human Rights Act.[17] The situation is included here to emphasize consideration of negligent retention concepts when processing sex harassment complaints against an employee and considering retention of the accused employee. In that circumstance, the likelihood of future negligent retention claims decreases if the accused is moved to another work site away from the complainant.

Defend against "negligent hiring" by reviewing your employment applications. Your applications should ask for references and enough personally identifiable information about each reference to at least allow phone checks.

1. Always do at least one *personal* reference check by phone on any applicant for employment, classified or certificated.

---

[17]*Geise v. Phoenix Co. of Chicago, Inc.*, 639 N.E. 2d 1273, 1277 (Ill. 1994).

2. Always do at least one *employment* check by phone on any applicant for employment, classified or certificated.

3. Intensify your checks on prospective employees with unexplained breaks in their employment history.

4. Whenever you receive an employment check that is too generic, intensify your investigation, for example, if you are told "He worked here from September 1988 to June 1990. He was assigned as a secondary classroom teacher. That's all I can tell you [or, I can't say any more than that] [or, that's all I want to say about him, etc.]."

5. Be suspicious of any employee who has worked for more than two prior K–12 school districts in this state or other states. When you see this pattern, check back beyond the last school employer.

6. Employment applications should ask the traditional: Have you been arrested or convicted or paid a fine for any infraction or any crime, except traffic infractions, during the past 5 [or 7] years?

7. Also ask about civil records that are pertinent to children: Have you been a party to any civil or criminal action involving injury to or dependency of a juvenile or had any child abuse complaint made against you?

8. Any applicant who makes any sort of qualified response to questions such as those suggested in 6 and 7 above, should be thoroughly investigated or refused hire.

IMPACT OF CIVIL LITIGATION

Historically, school boards controlled the management of local school districts. Now, a fair measure of "control" has passed to trial lawyers who prey on weak school administrators who cause or contribute to TSAS claims by students. In the process, because most suits claiming sexual harassment of students by staff are settled, and because the insured often cannot prohibit settlement by the insurer, control has also passed to school district liability insurance carriers and adjusters. Typically, settlement is built around a "release," in which the school district and named administrators, while denying any responsibility, pay out substantial sums of money to the plaintiff and his or her attorneys.

Usually, when there is litigation over sexual abuse, claims are made against the K–12 administrator in his/her *official* capacity, and claims are also made against him or her in a *private* or *personal* capacity. The official capacity claim is one alleging that the errant administrator acted within the scope of his/her employment; the private or personal capacity claim is one alleging that the administrator acted outside the scope of employment. Usually, the official capacity claim is insured against by the school district, but the private capacity claim is not. Therefore, the administrator is forced to make a claim against private insurance coverage, such as homeowner's insurance, and when claims are made, rates go up.

CHAPTER 8

Investigative Techniques and Considerations[18]

INTRODUCTION

ALTHOUGH K–12 school districts do not normally have trained investigators on staff, school districts have a duty to protect the health, safety, and welfare of enrolled students. The duty to act to avoid injury begins when possible risk can be foreseen, and in order to be proactive at that juncture, investigation becomes a necessary component of the K–12 educational process. Unfortunately, the K–12 administrator is increasingly called upon to investigate sexual exploitation of students.[19] Failure to train administrators in these processes can result in "deliberate indifference" tort claims which, in some cases, may be brought against administrators personally.

This chapter focuses on the K–12 administrator's role as an investigator: what should be investigated and what should not; what should be turned over to others and when. The following is not, however, intended to offer any sort of comprehensive training in investigative techniques or even considerations. The following is only an outline of investigative considerations especially applicable to sexual exploitation of students. For a detailed study see either "Investigating Alleged Wrongdoing by Employees in the School Setting" (R. Bump, et al., *School in*

[18]This chapter is authored by Mr. Biggs.
[19]See "School District Liability for Negligent Hiring and Retention of Unfit Employees," B. Beeper, ed., 56 Ed. Law Reporter. 117 (1990); *Sexual Harassment in the Schools' Preventing and Defending Against Claims,* NSBA Council of School Attorneys, National School Boards Association (1990).

Review, published by the National School Boards Association, Council of School Attorneys), or *School Administrator's Comprehensive Guide to Investigations* (J. Biggs).

Currently, this area of the law seems especially confused. The term "sexual harassment" is no longer a generic self-defining term. It includes "hostile educational environment sexual harassment," "hostile work environment harassment," "*quid pro quo* harassment," "teacher–student harassment," and "peer to peer harassment." However, it does not include criminal misconduct such as involuntary sexual intercourse, voluntary sexual intercourse with a person who is not old enough to voluntarily consent, indecent liberties, carnal knowledge, or communication with a minor for immoral purposes. Often, but not always, TSAS will engage in inappropriate touching or sexually gratifying conduct or inherently harmful conduct that rises to the level of criminal misconduct. In some cases, the criminal misconduct is mischaracterized as sexual harassment. In others, sexual harassment is mischaracterized as criminal misconduct. Altogether, because they are confusing to many K–12 administrators, these competing civil and criminal concepts have tended to aid the TSAS. At the same time, lawyers representing the victims have felt increasingly free to criticize action or inaction.

DEALING WITH LAW ENFORCEMENT

Deferring to Law Enforcement Investigation: The Good and Bad of It

Often (but not always), when possible sexual exploitation of a student by a teacher is at issue, a responsible law enforcement agency may be involved and may actively be investigating possible criminal misconduct. In this circumstance, the natural tendency of most K–12 administrators is to defer to these trained investigators, awaiting the outcome of the law enforcement investigation. Ideally, this investigation will result in exoneration of the accused or referral to prosecution, which leads to charges and then conviction for criminal activity involving students. Then, the administrator's role is to react by referring the miscreant teacher to professional certification at the state level and by basing a dismissal decision on the outcome of the criminal law processes. Unfortunately, however, proceeding in this manner is almost always a bad idea.

The Criminal Standard, Civil Standard Conundrum

The criminal evidentiary standard is "proof beyond a reasonable doubt" and the civil evidentiary standard is "preponderance of evidence," or "more likely than not." The criminal standard is higher, meaning someone (O.J. Simpson, for example) can be found "not guilty" under the criminal standard and "guilty" under the civil standard. The civil standard applies to the dismissal decision (employee retention). Thus, when we defer to a law enforcement investigation, we are deferring to a higher standard than actually applies to dismissal. Also, while a criminal defendant is entitled to a "speedy trial," society is not. Criminal processes grind slowly and a well-represented teacher-defendant can usually find ways to make sure the trial does not come quickly. When, as usual, the teacher is being paid a salary pending trial, continuances and delays become the order of the day. Thus, deferring to law enforcement can be a ticket to long-term delay. But, those considerations pale when compared to the fact that law enforcement usually cannot tell school administrators what was learned during the criminal investigation. Police agency disclosure to the school (a non-police agency) will usually violate the suspect's right to privacy. Most states have a "criminal records privacy act" which protects the rights of the criminal suspect and allows the suspect to control release of the investigative work-product to agencies or persons not related to law enforcement, and schools are not police agencies. Therefore, deferring to law enforcement is usually a bad idea, simply because the law enforcement agency usually cannot legally tell schools what was learned by law enforcement! Pretty amazing, isn't it?

The Civil Law, Criminal Law Lynch Pin

When the K–12 administrator has reasonable cause to believe that retention of a teacher in teacher–student contact represents foreseeable risk to students, that is usually the point in time when a report to law enforcement or child protective services is legally required.[20] It is approximately at this same point in the due process sequence when law enforcement has probable cause to believe that a crime has been committed or that a search warrant ought to be issued. This is (see below) the same point in time when a prudent K–12 administrator should cease internal agency investigation and call for an outside investigation.

There are two especially vexing problems when these particular worlds begin to collide: First, it will happen at the worst possible time, usually just as school is dismissed for the weekend or vacation when senior administrators are unavailable, thus forcing a decision by a junior administrator. The decision regarding whether or not to report to law enforcement and/or child protection agencies is a tough one. You can never be sure what action the responsible agencies will take and who will be believed; often the affected employee and his union are suggesting you are about to ruin a career and will surely pay for it. Report. Always err on the side of reporting. Whenever someone insists on talking you out of it, that is a good sign you ought to report. Every state has laws or case law that protects a person who is making a good faith report. When possible, find the school attorney; remember however, the duty to report is personal and you cannot relieve yourself of it by informing a superior or the attorney.

What to Do When Criminal Misconduct Is Suspected

First report, then get out of the way, then get to work. Most states have a law requiring that serious misconduct be reported. Err on the side of reporting. All states have a law that precludes "obstruction of justice," meaning interference with law enforcement investigation. Thus, when law enforcement

---

[20]See, for example, Revised Code of Washington where RCW 26.44.030 requires "reasonable cause to believe" report within forty-eight clock hours of reaching this conclusion.

wishes to investigate, K–12 must defer to law enforcement by facilitating and assisting the law enforcement investigation. These concepts do not mean we should do nothing, and, as indicated above, doing nothing is usually a bad idea. Therefore, once we have reported and done what can be done to assist the law enforcement investigation, it is usually time to begin our own parallel investigation. It is also time to recognize that what law enforcement is investigating is not, literally, the same thing we are investigating. For example, if a teacher is suspected of having improperly touched or fondled a student, law enforcement will be investigating elements of a criminal statute, e.g., were genitals touched? Was there sexual gratification? Was there consent? Meanwhile the school ought to conduct a parallel investigation of the following: Was there an educational purpose? Was the touching inherently harmful? Was the teacher in a supervisor role and more than five years older than the student? Whatever we do must be done parallel to and not in conflict with law enforcement, and our investigative work-product ought to be gratuitously offered to law enforcement, even if they have not asked for it, even if they do not really want it, and even if law enforcement is not reciprocating by sharing what they have learned. In order to know the elements of the misconduct you are investigating, you need a consultation with your school attorney. Ask how far into the past you ought to go, ask about looking at the employee's home life, ask about what sources can be used, and ask what you should do with and about coordination with law enforcement.

PREPARING TO INVESTIGATE

Develop an Investigative Outline

Know what you are going to begin investigating. For example, if Source A has reported that Teacher B fondled Student C, you are going to begin an investigation of possible fondling. But, that does not mean you are going to limit this search to Student C. Comments in the paragraph immediately above are reiterated here. You need to confer with the school attorney about this.

Who Is the Investigator? Who Is in Charge?

Generally, a school administrator is doing the initial investigation. Ideally, this is done under the supervision of someone who is disinterested and well-informed—usually the school attorney.[21] When sexual abuse allegations are made, everyone seems to be interested and to have some reason to be kept informed. Beware of this interest becoming an effort to control the investigation. The best case control officer is always someone who is as detached from or disinterested in the case as possible. Therefore, the superintendent or school board is almost always the worst possible case control officer.

When Should the Investigation Be Conducted?

Claims of sexual molestation, sexual abuse of students, or consensual sexual intercourse with students should take priority over everything else on your calendar. Change the planned trip or presentation; change the plans to observe and evaluate staff. The worst thing the assigned investigator can do is nothing, or, after beginning, delay in bringing the matter to closure. Starting is hard and, unfortunately, a good place to dither about what to do first. Ideally (see next section) you begin with the complainant but, beginning with anyone or anything is far more important than how you cast the scene.

Where Do You Begin?

Usually you should begin with the recent complainant who brought the matter to your attention. But this is not always possible. In some cases, a complainant will claim abuse and then refuse further interviews, or law enforcement will ask (or direct) that the student not be interviewed, or some other circumstance will intervene. When this occurs, it is not a good reason to delay—go ahead anyway. Begin as close to the com-

---

[21]See "Investigating Alleged Wrongdoing by Employees in the School Setting," R. Bump et al., *School Law in Review,* National School Boards Association, Council of School Attorneys; an excellent monograph that recommends that the school attorney act as case control officer.

plainant as possible. For example, if other students observed that the complainant's facial features suggested distress or heard or saw the complainant crying or heard the complainant make some emotional outburst, e.g., "I wish he'd leave me alone!," start with them. Again, starting is hard, but starting is far more important than where you start. A good thorough investigation will come out the same no matter where you start. I do recommend, though, that you not start with the alleged suspect. He or she is usually interviewed late or last in the process.

Seek Consensus Regarding the Objective

Investigation presents an opportunity for key personnel to never quite agree on what the investigative objective is. The school board may be intent on not being sued, the superintendent on getting rid of the teacher being investigated or avoiding some past event wherein action probably ought to have been taken, and the complainant on being allowed to go to school in an environment free of sexual abuse. Meanwhile, the investigator's objective must be to promptly assess foreseeable risk to student health, safety, and welfare.

THE TWO-TIER INVESTIGATIVE PROCESS

Method Explained

This approach presumes that the first-tier, initial, or preliminary investigation is done by a school administrator employed by the same school district that is being investigated.[22] This preliminary investigation is intended to rule in or rule out reasonable cause to believe or probable cause to believe (essentially synonymous terms) that abuse *may* have occurred. *Note:* the investigation is not intended to rule in or rule out that abuse *has* occurred; and there is a difference. The process plays

---

[22]This is the method required in Iowa. See "Procedures for Charging and Investigating Incidents of Abuse of Students by School Employees." Iowa Administrative Code 281:102 (256).

out with inherent presumptions. First, any internal investigation of an agency by agency itself is suspect. Second, any internal investigation of an agency, which is controlled or managed by someone within the agency, is suspect. Third, whenever an agency investigates itself and finds little or nothing, but some patron or investigator comes along later and finds out there was something there all along, that proves the first and second presumptions were well-taken. In the Nevada case, for example (see Case 10 in Chapter 3), a fed-up parent investigated and found victims and sources to prove twenty-two years of abuse; imagine what that said about the careers of the administrators who were supervising during that time. Imagine yourself in the same situation.

With the two-tier approach, when the preliminary investigation (first tier) fails to rule out abuse, it is time to bring in a trained outside investigator, or at least make certain that the case control officer (e.g., school attorney) is a disinterested person who will operate independently of the chief executive officers and school board. When possible criminal misconduct is reported to law enforcement or possible professional misconduct is reported to your state education agency, you are probably at this point. Always consult your school attorney.[23]

Unanticipated Early Referral

When using the two-tier method always consider that referral to an outside investigator takes precedence over use of a "collection phase" and a "response phase" (see "Conducting the Investigation" below). Err in favor of early referral to the second tier—the trained investigator. This may often occur before the "response phase" is reached, and if so, the trained investigator can later offer a "response phase."

When there is a pending law enforcement investigation of the same event(s) or when criminal misconduct is charged, finish the first-tier investigation and make the referral to the

[23]See "Children: When Teachers Sexually Abuse Children: The School District's Duty to Investigate," M. Miller, 43 *Oklahoma Law Review,* 687–704., e.g. "Once a level of heightened suspicion is reached, the school official should be aware that inaction may be considered condoning sexual abuse" (p. 703).

trained investigator. Similarly, make the referral when the first-tier investigation reveals other victims of sufficiently similar misconduct to provide evidence of a repetitive pattern, regardless of whether those other victims are in your school district or in districts where the employee worked earlier, and consider those other events as corroborating the present victim's contentions.

Routine First-Tier Referral to Decision Maker

Referral to the investigation to the decision-maker *may* occur following a brief first-tier collection phase (see explanation, following). The complaintant/victim *must* have been interviewed in this series and the suspected offender *may* have also been interviewed, or volunteered a statement. This early submission normally occurs when the case control officer (usually the school attorney) concludes there is either sufficient reliable information to recommend the matter be referred to a second-tier independent investigation. Developing another victim will, for example, dictate this result. Alternatively, the investigator may conclude there is insufficient reliable information to justify further investigation and no probability of developing it. Thus, the recommendation is to abort the investigation altogether. For example, the complaintant refuting his or her earlier statement and withdrawing complaint, may lead to this result.

CONDUCTING THE INVESTIGATION

A K–12 investigation involving possible employee misconduct usually has two distinct phases, the *collection phase* and the *response phase*. During the collection phase, the investigator gathers evidence about a circumstance or event. During the response phase, the suspected employee is given an opportunity to comment about the evidence gathered during the collection phase. This is presuming that a complete investigation is being conducted. However, as indicated above, when dealing with sexual abuse or misconduct, use of the two-tier method is preferred. Also, the manner in which a sexual harassment investigation (see below) is usually conducted is a bit different, there being a *comment phase* when the complainant is usually summarily briefed on the investigation and the investigator or decision maker's tentative decisions. Yet, recommended investigative methods (see below) are essentially the same for all these various types of investigations.

The Collection Phase

The Complainant and Alleged Victim(s)

Often, the victim and complainant is a female student. But in some cases, the complainant might be another student, a caring friend, or a parent. Listen and learn. Make a tentative outline of who is complaining, who is not, and who the alleged victim is.

Interviewing the Alleged Victim

Be in no hurry to gather facts. Focus instead on putting the source at ease. Choose an interview location that is comfortable to the victim, preferably not your office, and not during school with other students around. Be prepared to go to the victim's home, and if a parent or an older sibling insists on being present during the interview, allow that.

Avoid Structure

Use as little structure as possible. Tape recorders and camcorders are intimidating. A secretary inputting data into a computer during the interview is also intimidating. Questions beginning with "why" are often perceived as challenging and thus intimidating; for example, using questions such as "Why did you wait so long to report?" or "Why didn't you tell your mother?" or "Why didn't you tell him to stop?" etc. Similarly, use of preplanned questions and verbatim questions are not only intimidating but tend to narrow the focus rather than broaden it.

Maintain a Third-Person Witness

Always have someone else present. This may be an associate from the school or the school attorney, but it may also be the alleged victim's sibling, parent, or friend. Avoid being alone with the source. When this cannot be avoided, leave the door to the interview room open or choose a counselor- or coach-type office or room with a window to a common area.

Watch and Listen

Listen closely to what the victim is saying and formulate questions around and in response. Remember, the victim knows more about what happened than you do. Your purpose is to draw out, not stifle. Your purpose is to learn what there is to be learned. Pay attention to what the victim says and how he or she says it. Watch facial inflections and mannerisms. A victim wringing her hands while she talks is saying something with her hands. Plumb the depth of those feelings. They are your barometer of emotional and psychological damage and also an indicator of truthfulness.

Exhibit Empathy

Do not be put off by an angry or abrupt victim. Usually, the victim has already been interviewed, perhaps repetitively. These interviews may have been conducted by the family's lawyer, law enforcement, and child protective services, and, in some cases, by all of them. The victim is tired of talking about it and usually embarrassed.

Do Not Make Outcome Commitments

Avoid commitments to act toward an alleged miscreant in a certain way. Victims of sexual abuse or exploitation often just want it to stop, but they do not necessarily want the alleged abuser punished. In some cases they want him or her to be given counseling or a warning and nothing more. They will often want assurances of certain action or inaction in return for talking about the situation. Listen for the alleged victim's depth of feeling toward the abuser, but assume that the victim's feelings toward this person will probably change as events progress.

Complainant Not Necessarily Obligated to Testify

Do not insist that the alleged victim promise to testify against the actor. When there seems to be some doubt about that issue, bring it up on your own and assure the victim that he or she is making no commitment to testify. Talk about what will happen next. Put names to positions. If, for example, you will be reporting to the personnel director or superintendent, use a name. Describe as much as possible about what will happen next. A source, especially a victim, who learns more than he or she knew going into the interview, is usually inclined to continue association with you and submit to re-interviews.

Preserving Complainant's Report

I prefer to do witness summaries. These are fairly detailed reports on what the witness, including the victim, says happened. But these are not sworn statements or even necessarily signed statements.[24] All an audiotape, videotape, affidavit, declaration, or sworn statement does is prove the victim said what is contained in that record. Ask yourself if that is needed and ask yourself why. If you do not know, ask the school attorney. Usually, asking the victim to make a statement will put the victim off. It says you do not trust them and it says that they suddenly have to remember everything that happened. Victims of sexual exploitation and abuse have usually tried hard to forget and generally do not like to be faced with finally and completely having to remember everything, and usually they do not. A typical victim will change the report of what happened, often repeatedly. One event will become four and then twenty, one location will become several, etc. Insisting on

[24]The NSBA Council of School Attorneys recommends a written victim statement. See monograph at footnote 19.

an early statement tends to stifle that process. Earning the victim's trust will usually pay far greater dividends.

Developing Other Sources

As the victim details events, try hard not to interrupt, because when you do that, you are interrupting a thought process. But listen for "throw-off sources." These are others who can perhaps corroborate or refute the victim's report. They often are not identified by name, e.g., "After we were done, he stopped by the gas station in Taylor and bought us some soup and sandwiches." That is something you will want to go back to later in the interview after the thought is exhausted. An attendant at that station may recall seeing the victim and actor together in the vehicle. Often, people are only identified by first name, e.g., "we stopped by Susan's, she was babysitting and Ed called while we were there." You do not need to interrupt those sorts of comments. You can ask later who Susan is and if need be, Susan can tell you who Ed is.

Always ask the victim who else you should talk to. Then, encourage the victim to add to that list whenever he/she recalls anyone else. But remember, these are persons suggested by a disputant. Expect them to agree with the victim. Expect them to expect to be interviewed. These sources are important but they are not as important as a throw-off (see above) that no one had specifically identified as someone to be interviewed.

Being Open to New Leads

Listen for new and perhaps unexpected leads. For example, if the victim says, "My friend Mary said she wasn't surprised; her sister in college told her that there had been rumors years ago." You will now want to determine who Mary's sister is and interview her. Be prepared to expand the investigation to include new victims, some of whom may not previously have been known and some who may wish never to be known. Finding other victims is pattern evidence that tends to circumstantially corroborate the current complaint and perhaps classification of the current victim; for example, finding a then fourteen-year old blond cheerleader victim from three years ago certainly ought to add credence to the current fourteen-year-old blond cheerleader's claims.

Adjust Interview Techniques to Age of Source and Topic

When the source is a young child, meaning one at the fourth-grade level or below, and when the topic involves sexual abuse, various special considerations must be addressed. A general outline follows.

(1) Sexual Abuse, Grades Four and Below: What follows are guidelines for dealing with prepubescent children of the typical physical and emotional development levels found in grades K–4. But, there are no hard and fast rules. Some children mature more quickly and will respond more positively to the guidelines suggested for grades five through six. The first choice is always to notify your state child protective service agency (CPS), and until CPS has either interviewed or deferred, do not interview. However, when an interview cannot be avoided (meaning the child insists on telling his or her story now), proceed with the interview in a quiet place where interruptions won't occur. In the event the interviewer is not of the same sex as the child, ask a staff member of the same sex as the child, whom the child has associated with at school, to come in. Block out at least forty-five minutes.

1. During the interview process, allow the child to lead the interview, especially since the child may become emotional. In any event, the interviewer will normally be dealing with spontaneous utterances. These may take the form of incoherent sentences or repetitive references to a person or event.
2. In this situation, the administrator's primary duty is to observe and make a record of what the child says and how he or she says it, including mannerisms and emotional manifestations. These may take various forms, e.g., crying, tears without crying, red face or blushing, stuttering, incoherent speech, unresponsive speech, wringing hands, cracking knuckles, crossing and recrossing legs, wiggling, etc.
3. You may follow up on what the child says but should avoid

general exploratory questioning. If, for example, the child says, "and then he, he, looked at her and he lifted her dress . . . ," you would follow up by asking who "he" was and when and where this occurred. You would *not* ask, for example, "Have you ever seen anyone else do that to her?" Do not interrupt a distraught child who is in the process of opening up; save the follow-up questions until after the child finishes his or her story.

4. The administrator's secondary duty is to be supportive. Provide the child with a secure place and your attention. Reinforce the child. Avoid passing judgment on what is being said or whether gestures or facial expressions are consistently saying it.

5. Meanwhile, initiate efforts to contact the child's parents and let them know what is going on. Have this done by another staff person rather than interrupting the interview to do it yourself. When you know or suspect that the child has not related the same facts to the parent, be prepared to support the child during the meeting—expect a child source to be fearful of the parent's reaction. If you don't know what the parent has been told, then after the child is finished with his or her recitation, ask if the parent knows; ask if the child is concerned about telling the parent; offer your services to the child.

6. When the child is emotionally upset, do not return the child directly to the classroom. Put the child in the infirmary and have someone monitor the child until the parents arrive. Whoever is monitoring should especially watch for emotional difficulties of the sort described above. After the child has been delivered to the parent this person should do a memo on what he or she observed.

7. In the event the child has related facts (new information) indicating that he or she observed possible abuse of another child, supplement earlier reports to Child Protective Services or law enforcement immediately after finishing the interview.

(2) Sexual Abuse Claims, Grades Five through Six: The

procedures for handling a witness and handling a victim are the same as outlined above. However, the age and maturity levels of the child have increased. At this level the administrator is normally dealing with children who have some understanding of the physical and emotional changes that go with puberty. Girls at this level are often familiar with the growth of pubic hair, breast development, and the meaning of the term *intercourse.* They often have fixed opinions as to what is and is not a private part of the body. Boys at this age level are becoming familiar with the meaning of intercourse, penile erection, and ejaculation. Even boys who have not yet begun to undergo the physical changes associated with puberty tend to have more fixed opinions about what is good touching and what is bad touching.

Therefore, there is an opportunity at this level to engage in a more detailed discussion of what was observed or what has occurred. Usually however, the use of anatomical dolls is contraindicated at this level and some students of this age will be offended by their use.

Also, in our experience, students at this level begin to judge the level of interest shown by the interviewer by the length of time taken with them or with follow-up questioning. Unlike younger children, students in this age group may very well expect you to use questions beginning with "did" or "could" or "do."

Like the younger children, sources at this level should not be asked questions eliciting a "yes" or "no" answer. Observation of mannerisms and emotional responses is just as important as it is when dealing with younger children. Avoiding judgmental facial expressions or mannerisms is also important with this age group, and, in some cases, even more important.

(3) Sexual Abuse Claims, Grades Seven and Above: Students at this level generally expect to be treated as adults. They do, however, become emotional when blurting out a story and they may feel compelled to tell to someone. In addition to the considerations outlined above, students at this age tend to inquire. They want to know what is going to happen to them, what is going to happen to the alleged abuser, what the police will do, etc., etc. Attempt to answer their questions or refer

them to whoever can answer. At this age especially, a source who has learned something new during the interview is likely to remain a cooperative source as time goes by.

Investigate Based on Health and Safety Needs, Not Only What Is Complained About

In some cases, a parent or child or patron will make a complaint that deserves investigation. But, the investigator must remain free to focus attention on matters other than those complained about. For example, the following letter was received by a small rural school board:

> School board members and Superintendent of [BLANK]
>
> We are submitting this letter of concern about the unhealthy attitude and actions of the fifth and sixth grade teacher, [BLANK TEACHER].
>
> As parent of students in the [BLANK] school system and two children under direct supervision of this teacher, we feel that his obsession with a student ([BLANK]) is beyond the role of a teacher and points more to that of an infatuated person. We feel that this environment is not of a moral standard accepted by us and creates an unhealthy atmosphere.
>
> We feel that the credibility of this teacher has fallen! When our children are asked to leave the classroom to check on [BLANK STUDENT] and carry personal notes from [BLANK TEACHER] this takes valuable learning away from their education.

This complaint began the investigation of Orville Longuskie (see Case 9 in Chapter 3). Mr. Longuskie was a homosexual pedophile who was sexually abusing a young male student. Note that the initial complaint neither mentioned nor even considered sexual abuse.

Investigating Private Life or Activities

Always consult the school attorney before investigating an employee's private life activities. Sufficient reliable information to believe there is a connection (nexus) between private life and foreseeable risk at school is a precondition. Expect the choice to investigate to be held to a higher standard than that which applies to work-related investigative choices. The following case illustrates both what is relevant and what is not relevant to this choice.

A middle school administrator, who belonged to and followed the tenets of a fundamental religious denomination, suspected a female teacher was intimately involved with a male student. The administrator called both the student and the teacher (separately) into his office and questioned them about their relationship with each other. Both denied an improper relationship existed. About a year later, the male student reported that he'd had sexual intercourse with the teacher. When this complaint was made, the superintendent commissioned an outside investigation. The teacher denied the charge. The middle school administrator opined that the student's description of events was probably true. The following are the various reasons why the middle school administrator believed that the incidents reported by the student had, in fact, taken place:

1. Although the teacher was in her mid-thirties, she dressed as if she were in her early twenties.
2. The teacher worked part-time as a waitress at a local bar.
3. The teacher was single.
4. The teacher reportedly enjoyed watching X-rated movies with a male friend her age.
5. The teacher drove a sports car.
6. Years earlier, the student had run away from home and lived for a few weeks in a car.
7. The teacher had drawn a suggestive cartoon for the student.
8. The teacher had asked the student to mow her lawn and he did so on several occasions. As a result, the two were often alone away from school.
9. The teacher had given the student a bike.
10. The teacher had given the student a leather bomber jacket.
11. The teacher and student had been observed dancing with each other at a Valentine's Day dance.
12. The student had told a fellow student, at about the time of

the alleged sexual intercourse, that he'd had intercourse with the teacher.

13. In his description of sexual encounters at the teacher's home, the student described various furnishings and facts particular to the home and various rooms in the home, including the teacher's bedroom.

In the above list, items 7 through 13 are legitimate factual bases to suspect that this teacher possibly had an intimate relationship with her student that was not acceptable. However, in and of themselves, items 1 through 6 are not good reasons to investigate the private life of an employee. Their inclusion in the list represents a comment as to what the source considers "unacceptable" conduct or conduct suggesting something else altogether. The foregoing is an actual event from the Sheila and Carl scenario (see Case 10 in Chapter 3).

Continually Separate Relevant Evidence from Irrelevant Evidence

The following scenario is an example of how to handle extraneous evidence: This investigation involved an elementary-level PE specialist. Female fifth-grade students had suggested that this particular teacher "looks down my blouse" and "looks up my dress." One girl complained, "it felt 'funny' when he touched my bottom to help me up the climbing rope."

Note how subjective these complaints are. PE specialists are expected to help kids climb ropes. PE specialists often are in situations that can be misconstrued by this particular age group, boys or girls. However, if in fact this employee was making his female students feel uncomfortable, he was engaging in a form of subtle and perhaps unintentional sexual harassment. If he were actually seeking sexual gratification from conduct of the sort described by the students he would have to be removed from student contact. There is no legitimate educational purpose to any sort of sexually gratifying conduct between a teacher and student.

However, as the investigation proceeded it was obvious that

there were a variety of complaints against this particular teacher. The following complaints were noted:

1. When we bring cookies or cake for the teacher's room, he eats all of it!
2. He doesn't bathe often enough—he stinks!
3. He's fat and all of his PE clothes are about three sizes too small and rolls of fat stick out!
4. He's stolen lunch tickets. We have to pay for them and he shouldn't be allowed to get away with that!
5. He has boys at home and they're kind of weird. Once, one of them urinated off the roof of the house.
6. He calls his wife all the time during school when he should be supervising students.

Facts 1 through 6 have nothing to do with little girls' complaints about possibly leering down a blouse or up a skirt. Put another way, just because someone is an unkempt slob, it doesn't follow that he's a pervert. However, the complaints are marginally relevant as commentaries on the source's motive. The foregoing are comments made by fellow teachers about a teacher, and from those comments it was obvious these folks weren't fond of this fellow.

Winding Up the Collection Phase

The investigator's notes ought to be used as the basis to prepare witness summaries that detail what the witness said. These summaries should not, however, include the investigator's impressions of the witness's demeanor or credibility—only what the witness said. If, for example, the witness insisted that the moon is made of green cheese, that ought to be reported. These summaries, plus whatever other evidence is available, copies of love letters to or from the teacher, for example, or copies of e-mail retrieved from e-mail archives, etc., are then provided to the suspected employee. This is usually done through the employee's association representative or legal counsel, but the documentation can be provided directly to the employee. Normally, whatever information can be submitted to the decision maker on discipline should be submitted to the employee for possible comment.

Response Phase

Employees who are suspected of having been involved in sexual abuse or exploitation of children, or who have a history suggesting future risk to student health, safety, and welfare, must be provided with due process of law. However, the term itself is not generic; there is *procedural due process* and there is *substantive due process*. These terms may, at times overlap. Procedural due process is dependent upon state law, local school district policies and procedures and, in some cases, collective bargaining agreements with employee unions or associations. Always seek legal advice as to what your local *procedural* due process requirements are.

The term *substantive due process* refers to the appearance of fairness and the basic fairness of the process being used. For example, in many cases it is unfair to investigate by interviewing only witnesses who dislike the person being investigated or to ignore witnesses who will report mitigating circumstances such as a suspect's drug or alcohol dependency or dislocation in the suspect's domestic affairs.

In the context of the "response phase," substantive due process generally requires that we give the suspected employee notice of all the information that may lead to adverse action against the employee, including dismissal. We do this by either providing the suspected employee or employee's labor or legal representative with copies of witness summaries collected during the "collection phase," or briefing the suspected employee on this information. Then, the suspected employee should be given a reasonable opportunity to respond. This is commonly referred to as the "predetermination" or "pretermination" meeting or opportunity. However, while due process requires that we offer the employee the opportunity to respond, it does not require that the employee actually respond. The form of response is usually legally immaterial; the employee can respond orally or in writing, the employee can respond in person or by his or her labor or legal representative. Because the "predetermination" opportunity is intended to avoid some easily avoidable mistake, the reasonable time to respond is generally only a day or two at this level. Later, if the employee receives a notice of dismissal and requests a hearing, your procedural due process will provide the employee more time and, substantive due process will also then require more time.

In some cases, this "predetermination" or "pretermination" process must be repeated two or more times. This can occur when the "collection phase" exceeds about ten calendar days in length. When it is obvious that this is probably going to occur, I recommend a preliminary "predetermination" opportunity followed later by another as to information developed after the first such opportunity. The employee being investigated can, however, elect to wait until the entire investigation is completed and exercise the "predetermination" opportunity at one time.

SEXUAL HARASSMENT INVESTIGATION IN THE K–12 SCHOOL SETTING

Most TSAS situations involve an adult male teacher and a female student. Also, most TSAS incidents occur at the secondary level, meaning grades six through twelve. Coincidentally, most (but not all) of the considerations applicable to sexual harassment investigation apply to these situations. Therefore the following primer on sexual harassment investigation is included here.

Sexual Harassment Defined

Before you investigate sexual harassment, make sure you know what it means and what it is. For example, do you know what *quid pro quo* harassment is? Do you know what hostile educational environment or hostile work environment sexual harassment is? Do you know the differences between sexual harassment standards applicable to possible harassment of an adult by an adult and possible sexual harassment of a student by a student? Is touching of a student sexual harassment, assault, or both? Is the touching of a student's private areas sexual harassment or carnal knowledge? Do you know?

A good general definition of what is actionable in schools is found in the Washington State statutes at RCW 28A.640.020(2)(f):

> "Sexual harassment" . . . means unwelcome sexual advances, requests for sexual favors, sexually motivated physical contact, or other verbal or physical conduct or communication of a sexual nature if:
>
> (i) Submission to that conduct or communication is made a term or condition, either explicitly or implicitly, of obtaining an education or employment;
>
> (ii) Submission to or rejection of that conduct or communication by an individual is used as a factor in decisions affecting that individual's education or employment; or
>
> (iii) That conduct or communication has the purpose or effect of substantially interfering with an individual's educational or work performance, or of creating an intimidating, hostile, or offensive educational or work environment.

Sexual harassment is a national problem and you will find any state-law definition of sex harassment consistent with the foregoing quote. Confusion does arise though from application of *welcomeness,* which is an *adult-to-adult* concept. That concept should never excuse ". . . verbal or physical conduct or communication of a sexual nature. . . ." between a staff member and a K–12 student. In part this confusion arises because at the college level, where students are generally all over 18 years of age, and thus entitled to *welcome* advances by a staff member if they wish, the same restrictions do not apply.

An otherwise offensive remark is not necessarily actionable sex harassment. Also, *between two adults,* rude, crude, or vulgar comments, even if unwelcome, may not be severe enough or pervasive enough to create a hostile work environment. In the K–12 educational environment, the foregoing rules may apply to the adult staff persons' interactions with each other. In the college-level educational environment, most (but not all) the foregoing rules apply to student's interaction with staff. However, none of those *adult-to-adult* concepts apply to the educational environment relationship between an adult staff member and a K–12 student. What is potentially *welcome* interaction between adults is potentially unconscionable sexual "grooming" of a student. Similarly, in the K–12 educational environment, even when *adult-to-adult* interaction is *welcome* or when it is not rude, crude, or vulgar enough or pervasive enough to create an *adult-to-adult* hostile *work environment,* it may very well create a *hostile educational environment* for the student exposed to it or required to endure it. K–12 students have a right to be there; staff have a "privilege" to be there. Staff's privilege is conditioned on their not jeopardizing, either directly or indirectly, the health, safety or welfare of the students. See the Supreme Court decision in *Harris Forklift Systems, Inc.,* 126 L.Ed. 2d 295 (1993), at 302; See also Office of Civil Rights Letter Opinion to Eden Prairie Schools, April 27, 1993 (Complaint 05-92-1174) reprinted in "A Word On . . . ," Volume IX, No. 3, NSBA Office of The General Counsel, Summer, 1993:

> "A sexually hostile environment is created by acts of a sexual nature that are sufficiently severe or pervasive to impair the educational benefits offered by recipient. . . . In determining whether sexual harassment exposes students because of their sex to a hostile environment, relevant circumstances include the age of the victim(s); the frequency, duration, repetition, location, severity, and scope of the act(s) of harassment; the nature and context of the incident(s); whether the conduct was verbal or physical; whether others joined in perpetuating the alleged harassment; whether the harassment was directed at more than one person; and whether the alleged incidents created an offensive, hostile or abusive atmosphere at the district or at specific schools or in other district settings, such as school buses.

I therefore recommend that "hostile educational environment harassment," which is a version of hostile work environment harassment, be defined and evaluated by use of the following.

Elements of Sexual Harassment

1. Was the student subjected to unwelcome sexual harassment

in the form of sexual advances, requests for sexual favors, or other verbal or physical conduct of a sexual nature?

2. Was the harassment based upon the victim's sex? (Would the harassment have occurred if the victim were of the opposite sex?)

3. Did the harassment unreasonably interfere with the complainant's studies or his/her educational environment?

4. Was there a pattern of harassment or is the complaint based upon one isolated incident?

5. If there was a pattern, would a reasonable person of the same sex as the complainant have found the complainant's work environment to be intimidating, hostile, or offensive?

Types of Sexual Harassment That May Occur in the School Setting

Hostile Environment Sexual Harassment

In schools, requiring an employee to continue to serve in a sexually hostile or intimidating environment is "hostile work environment" sexual harassment and not "hostile educational environment" sexual harassment. This is the case even though the harassment occurs in an educational environment. The term "hostile educational environment sexual harassment" may refer to adult-to-student harassment. However, it is generally associated with adult-to-adult harassment and, for the most part, this form of sexual harassment is defined and governed by the same rules and regulations that apply to any work environment—not just schools. Because its genesis is in Section 703, Title VII, Civil Rights Act of 1964, implemented at 29 Code of Federal Regulations (CFR) 1604.11, this form of sexual harassment is often referred to as "Title VII harassment."

Correspondingly, requiring a student to continue learning in a hostile or intimidating environment is "hostile educational environment" sexual harassment. This is true whether the cause of the harassment is the actions or inactions of an adult staff member, a visitor, or a fellow student. This form of sexual harassment is defined and governed by rules and laws that apply only to students. Because its genesis is in Title IX, Educational Amendments of 1972, this form of sexual harassment is often referred to as "Title IX harassment."

Neither adult school employees nor students clearly understand the differences between Title VII harassment and Title IX harassment, because what is and what is not hostile educational environment sexual harassment varies much more than the variations found within hostile work environment sexual harassment. Title IX applies to both colleges and common schools; what is actionable sexual harassment of a fourth-grade girl may not be actionable sexual harassment of a twenty-one-year-old college student. When sexual harassment began to take effect as a definable form of discrimination, there was an effort to develop universally acceptable definitions. As to work environment, this effort continues and has been largely successful. In my opinion, continued attempts to find the universal definition have tended to do little more than add to K–12 administrators' existing confusion.

Quid Pro Quo *Harassment*

Quid pro quo is defined by the Equal Employment Opportunity Commission (EEOC) as:

> Unwelcome sexual advances, requests for sexual favors, and other verbal or physical conduct of a sexual nature constitute sexual harassment when:
>
> a. Submission to the verbal or physical harassment is made either explicitly or implicitly a term or condition of an individual's employment.
>
> b. Submission to or rejection of the verbal or physical harassment is used as a basis for employment decision affecting such an individual.

The perception of the victim is important but not determinative. Every investigation must evaluate whether the victim's perception is (a) accurate and (b) reasonable. An alleged victim of leering may, for example, accurately perceive a supervisor looking at his or her body but unreasonably perceive the look to be leering.

In schools, we protect employees from harassment by fellow employees, students, and others including officials such as board members, and visitors, such as a parent attending a parent–teacher conference. Similarly, we protect students from harassment by any school staff, classified or certificated, by fellow students, and by officials and by anyone who is invited into the educational setting or invades it.

Types of Sexual Harassment May Overlap in the Same Case

Sexual harassment is not a generic term. In the K–12 educational environment, it may refer to peer-to-peer harassment, to hostile work environment harassment, or to educational environment harassment. The term *quid pro quo* harassment also has varying meanings in the educational environment. It may refer to a supervisor–subordinate relationship, such as that between a principal and a teacher, or the relationship between a teacher and a student.

Handling Sexual Harassment Complaints

The procedural due process requirements applicable to processing these complaints abound. First, review your local school district's policies and procedures. Next, look at state laws and regulations. Next, review the Equal Employment Opportunity Commission's (EEOC) requirements relating to sexual harassment of an adult, or the United States Department of Education, Office of Civil Rights' (OCR) requirements applicable to Title IX sexual harassment of a student. Finally, always contact your school attorney for advice.

Processing a Sexual Harassment Complaint

Complaint processes usually require that a particular form, process, or both be used. However, focusing on these procedural requirements can tend to stifle complaints, and with sexual harassment, it is always best to encourage rather than discourage complaints. In some cases, because the employer can be held to have known about the harassment, no complaint is even necessary; therefore, insisting on or accepting only a particular type or form of complaint tends to make a bad situation worse. Knowing of offensive hostile work environment harassment is akin to "taking a complaint" [see *E.E.O.C. v. Hacienda Hotel,* 881 F. 2d 1504, 1515-1516 (9th Cir. 1989)]. Similarly, if, with reasonable care, the employer should have known of such a work-related condition, a complaint is unnecessary [see *Meritor Savings Bank v. Vinson,* 447 U.S. 57, 106 S. Ct. 2399, 91 L.Ed. 2d 49 (1986)]. On the other hand, when the employee interaction appears to be welcome, a complaint is appropriate. Taken together, these concepts suggest that we ought not always rely upon our sexual harassment complaint processes.

For example, if an employee or student voices a complaint but refuses to put that complaint in writing, case law suggests that the school district may still be held to know of the harassment condition [see *Intelkofer v. Turnage,* 973 F. 2d 773, 778 (9th Cir. 1992)]. Therefore, whether the formal complaint processes are used or not, I recommend that the possibly harassing condition be promptly investigated. Failure to do so may be alleged as basis for "deliberate indifference" to the injurious impact on the student.

What Does a Sexual Harassment Complaint Sound Like?

There is no standard form of complaint. Therefore, case law errs on the side of imposing a duty on the school to understand or appreciate what is being said. For example, an employee or student saying they are "uncomfortable" at work or school can be enough. A student saying "I never wear dresses to his class!" is probably enough. The sexual harassment complaint might be buried in a collection of grievances, most of which have nothing to do with sexual harassment. However, some complaints are too broad, using the term *harassment* to include gender-based harassment and poor collegiality among staff, or an abrupt business relationship between a supervisor and subordinate.

Schools should have both a Title VII and a Title IX compliance officer. Ideally, this is a person schooled in these federal laws and the Code of Federal Regulations (CFR) requirements developed from them. Also, ideally, the sexual harassment complainant would make his or her complaint to this compliance officer. But in practice, that rarely occurs. Instead, a building-level or mid-level manager or administrator often receives the complaint. He or she may not recognize it for what it is, but as a legal consequence of the communication, the school district will be held to know.

Who Should Investigate

Someone with some training in investigative techniques in general, or sexual harassment investigations in particular, is preferred. As a general rule, however, because this sort of investigation is not akin to investigation of criminal misconduct and because the of the intimidation factor, use of staff security personnel is not indicated. As a general rule, the investigator ought to come from the ranks of management and be at least from the same managerial level as the suspected harasser. When litigation is possible, the school attorney ought to be consulted before the investigation begins and always at least before it is concluded. In some cases, using a lawyer to investigate may be indicated, but if the lawyer later becomes a witness, he or she may not be allowed to represent the school district at trial or hearing. Union or employer representatives of the complainant, and sometimes the suspect, may demand the right to participate in the investigation, which as a general rule, is a bad idea. When that occurs, accept their objections and continue the investigation without them.

The Investigator Must Walk in the Shoes of the Complainant

In order to factor in age, maturity, setting, etc., and still retain some commonality, as a society we have continually attempted to redefine the level of offensiveness necessary to achieve actionable harassment. In the beginning, sexual harassment had to be offensive to a reasonable, prudent person.

However, because those of one gender will not necessarily appreciate the offensiveness of actions or inactions clearly offensive to the other gender, and because most victims of sex harassment are women, the Ninth Circuit Court of Appeals adopted the "reasonable woman" as its standard for determining harassment. Even though the "reasonable woman" standard works well in the work environment, it fails when applied to most K–12 students in Title IX sexual harassment cases because most female students in K–12 schools are juveniles. Thus, potentially harassing comments or events which may not be offensive to an adult female may very well be offensive to a juvenile female. Therefore, use the reasonable victim standard. When applying TNS standard, recognize our early case law required psychological damage, but most recently case law has clearly indicated that waiting until psychological damage has occurred is waiting too long.

The Reasonable Victim Test

In schools, Title IX sexual harassment is now tested by the "reasonable victim" standard. The "reasonable victim" can be a "reasonable male student" if the victim is male, or "reasonable female student" if the victim is female. The "reasonable victim" is supposed to be someone of the same sex and about the same age who attempts to function in the same environment. In evaluating hostile educational environment harassment, OCR applies the reasonable victim standard. In its letter to Eden Prairie Schools (see "Sex Harassment Defined," above) OCR applied this standard: "From the standpoint of a reasonable female student participating in district programs and activities in these locations, the sexually offensive conduct was sufficiently frequent, severe and/or protracted to impair significantly the educational services and benefits offered."

The following list of indices is based upon *The Lecherous Professor* by Dziech, B. W. (1990), Illini Books, Champaign, IL, which is a recommended resource when investigating hostile educational environment harassment.

What May Be Offensive and Thus Constitute Sexual Harassment

- staring, leering, ogling (whether surreptitious or obvious)

- frequently commenting on the personal appearance of a student
- touching out of context: Always ask, "What is the educational purpose?" associated with any touching. Touching, even touching which is not inherently harmful, is especially invasive. Therefore, the determination of whether a reasonable person would find unwanted or unwelcome touching intimidating, hostile, or offensive ought to be broadly applied.
- excessive flattery and praise of the student: This may be especially seductive to students with low self-esteem or high aspirations.
- Is the suspect deliberately seeking encounters with the victim?
- injecting a "male versus female" tone into discussions
- persistently emphasizing sexuality in all contexts

Here are some other examples of what has been found to be patently offensive to students:

- repeated complaints, by a secondary female student, about student-to-student harassment that resulted in no overt actions by the school administration, which had coincidentally failed to designate a Title IX compliance officer
- young elementary age boys repeatedly taunting a girl in front of others with the term "moo moo"
- a lack of prompt response to complaints by a female student about graffiti that referred to her as a "slut"
- at the fifth- and sixth-grade levels, repeated incidents of peer-to-peer lewd language, touching, pinching, and name-calling

In one situation, the perpetrators were students with special needs, classified in special education; OCR ruled that the school's deferring to these disabilities was not appropriate (see "A Legal Memorandum," National Association of Secondary School Principals, November, 1994). These sorts of issues may develop during an investigation of adult-to-student harassment. When they do, these other incidents ought to be investigated too. They may form part of a pattern and may also aggravate the injury to the student, caused by otherwise unrelated adult-to-student harassment in the same educational setting.

Investigative Considerations Applicable to Sexual Harassment

Fostering Openness during Investigation

Ask yourself, Where can I make the complainant and witnesses most at ease with this process? It may not be in the office, a place with phone interruptions and a large desk between the interviewer and source or complainant. When the source or complainant is not comfortable meeting in the work environment, attempt to meet at another location. But, especially with sources or complainants of student age, always avoid in-person solitary meetings. When phone interviewing is taking place, do not assume that the source knows who you are. When there is any indication that a source doubts your identity or authority, encourage the source to call you back through the school phone system. When doing in-person interviews of sources that do not know you, plan on having a letter of introduction from someone in the school that the source does know. Alternatively, have someone the source knows and trusts call ahead to introduce you as someone with the authority to conduct this sort of investigation.

Avoid Threatening or Challenging the Complainant or Sources

A sexual harassment investigator, regardless of his or her gender, is expected to judge offensiveness by the standard of the reasonable victim of the same sex, approximate age, and maturity [*Ellison v. Brady,* 924 F. 2d 878 (9th Cir. 1991)]. It should not be easy to make a sexual harassment complaint—and, it isn't. The investigator should be supportive and understanding. Comment on a complainant's answers or emotions by saying, "I appreciate that," "I understand," "This must be difficult," etc., exhibit an understanding of the difficulty the complainant is experiencing.

Similarly, questions to the complainant that are challenging in nature should be avoided when appropriate. Most questions beginning with "why" are challenging, e.g., "Why didn't you make this complaint earlier?" or "Why did you laugh at the dirty joke?"

Usually, "why" questions are always inappropriate during a first interview with a complainant, but are sometimes appropriate on re-interview. As a general rule, because of lower age and maturity, "why" questions are less appropriate with student complainants than adult complainants.

Jurisdictional Limits

Normally, we investigate only situations developing at school or school-related activities. But, there are exceptions. For example, in *Keppler v. Hinsdale Tp. High School Dist.* [715 F. Supp. 862 (N.D.Ill. 1989)], an evolving relationship is traced between two administrators. The relationship begins when one is an assistant principal and the other is a coordinator of educational services. But careers do not remain static and one becomes director of special education and the other a principal. Eventually, a *quid pro quo* situation arguably arose where one party exercised some supervisory control over the other. As between adults, in determining when sexual advances were welcome and later unwelcome, evidence of events occurring outside of school is often relevant. For example, in *Trautvetter v. Quick* [916 F. 2d 1140 (7th Cir. 1990)], evidence of events at school, at a hospital, in a parking lot, in a car, in a motel, etc., were all relevant to a sexaul harassment complaint.

When the situation possibly involves adult-to-student harassment, whether incidents occur at school or away from school, during the school year or during vacations or weekends, presume there is a connection (a nexus). In this circumstance, the questions are: "Is there any educational purpose to the contact?" "If the conduct occurred at school, would it be treated as inherently harmful?" and "Is the conduct a result of or related to association at school?"

In the situations presented above, there is a potential invasion of privacy issue. Therefore, incident to any investigation of private life, the school attorney ought to be consulted before extending the investigation to events away from school [see *Burns v. McGregor Electronic Industries, Inc.,* 989 F. 2d 959 (8th Cir. 1983)].

Retaliatory Discrimination

Public policy and the law stand against sexual harassment. A person who complains of sexual harassment is protected against any sort of retaliatory discrimination. A supervisor disadvantaging a subordinate who has made complaint in regard to any terms or conditions of employment, including activities protected by the school district's policies and procedures, is presumptively retaliating. This means the burden is then on the supervisor to prove that he or she did not retaliate.

Similarly, a teacher or staff person who somehow disadvantages a student as to grade, credit, or educational opportunity is presumptively retaliating and the burden is on the school district to prove that what occurred was not retaliation. These presumptions are not easily overcome. Therefore, early in any sexual harassment investigation, it is best to directly or indirectly communicate to the suspected offender that he or she ought not communicate with the complainant or engage in any sort of retaliatory activity. This can be done orally or in writing; it can be done directly and it can be done through the suspected person's labor representative.

When meeting with a suspected harasser who is an employee, and when there is any possibility of discussion with the suspect, exercise best efforts to see that the suspect has a labor representative present at the time of the meeting (see references to *Weingarten* in the section following).

The Two-Phase Investigative Process in Sexual Harassment Investigation

As a general rule, the investigator ought to collect information by interviewing the complainant and sources who agree or disagree (phase one), collating the information, presenting it to the suspected person, eliciting his/her response, if any, followed by submission of the investigation to the decision maker (person who decides disposition of complaint)(phase two). When possible, to maintain maximum objectivity, it is best if the investigator is not also the decision maker. With sexual harassment, it is almost always best to debrief the complainant—meaning that once the investigation is complete and the investigator is prepared to submit it and perhaps make a recommendation, the investigation ought to be summarized to the complainant. The proposed recommendation ought to be similarly summarized. When the investigator, in whole or in part, disagrees with the complainant, this is an uncomfortable process, which is exactly why it is recommended.

Sexual harassment investigations can be inconclusive. However, an investigation that is inconclusive regarding whether a particular event happened in a particular way or whether the suspect intended a certain consequence, is often conclusive as to the alleged victim's perception that harassment did, in fact, occur. In that circumstance, the suspected employee or student ought to be cautioned to avoid the actions that were perceived as harassing and warned that if the admonition is ignored, disciplinary action may follow. The investigation and the remedy must be reasonably calculated to end the harassment [*Waltman v. International Paper Co.,* 875 F. 2d 468, 479 (5th Cir. 1989); *Ellison v. Brady,* 924 F. 2d at 883]. When the harasser is a student, the discipline imposed must be reasonably calculated to end the harassment, and OCR expects the student's parents to be notified (OCR Letter Opinion, Eden Prairie Schools, OCR Complaint 05-92-1174).

In regard to disclosure to the complainant and others (public disclosure), a sexual harassment investigation is "preliminary" while in progress, but once the decision maker has decided what, if anything, to do, "preliminary" investigative status ceases and the investigation may be discloseable. Review state law.

When the investigation is being submitted to a suspected harasser who is an employee, there is a possibility of disadvantage to the suspect. Therefore, a labor representative ought to be included [see *NLRB v. Weingarten, Inc.,* 420 U.S. 251, 95 S. Ct. 959, 43 L.Ed. 2d 171 (1975)]. As a general rule, when the inquiry relates to a work-related situation and when the information requested is not going to form later basis for a criminal complaint, the suspected employee does have a duty to answer [*Gardner v. Broderick,* 392 U.S. 273, 88 S.Ct. 1913, 1916 (1968)]. In every case, the school attorney ought to be consulted before the suspected employee is interviewed.

Possible Defamation Action Against Complainant

School employees suspected of sexual harassment may respond by threatening to sue those staff or students complaining against them. In limited circumstances, these suits can be pursued. For example, when a work-related Title VII sexual harassment complaint is made by one employee against another, and when the suspect has proof that the complaint is false and the complainant knew the complaint was false, a suit may be possible [*Lawson v. Boeing Company,* 58 Wn. App. 261, 269, 792 P. 2d 545 (1990)]. The question of whether a school employee can sue a student bringing a Title IX complaint is uncertain.

However, when an employee or student makes a complaint that has even a scintilla of merit (any supporting evidence at all), public policy clearly favors the complainant over the accused. In this circumstance, the accused is precluded from bringing any sort of defamation or injury to reputation or business reputation claim against the accuser.

Recently, labor organizations have begun to attempt to preclude placement or insist upon removal of any complaint or file on possible sexual harassment, proven or not. Here, contract protections commonly found in collective bargaining agreements, such as a clause requiring removal of negative information within a specified period of time (e.g., two years) conflict with legal requirements to maintain a historical record of previous complaints. I recommend erring on the side of retention of the information.

A Wife's Account

THIS is the story of the wife of a teacher who, for many years, across many states, molested his female students. The man was a dedicated, hard-working teacher and coach. As we follow this case we can see how his family's life revolved around his teaching. We see a devoted wife who, after his first incident, remains devoted to him though she makes a suicide attempt. We gain insight into the educational system that allows him to resign and seek other teaching positions, without any adverse notices in his file. There is no treatment, and the teacher does not acknowledge his problem. The behavior does not end, though it ceases for some time. The geographical moves are suspicious, since I believe that most teachers are sedentary. As this man finds it difficult to find a teaching position he goes to work for a fast food restaurant. Most of the employees are teenagers. Again, we might assume that his sexual/personal motives are predominant in his career choices.

Eventually he secures another teaching position with coaching responsibilities. As my research indicates, it is coaches and teachers who engage in out-of-classroom, off-campus activities who are the most prone to commit sex offenses.

The wife looks back on the victims and notices that they were troubled kids. The molester is selective and "lures" or "grooms" the victims. What may have just happened in the first case no longer is an accident. The teacher develops a style and, has well-honed procedures and lies to cover his activities. At times, teachers endear themselves to parents and school administrators so there won't be any suspicion. In this case the teacher doesn't seek counseling and doesn't acknowledge a problem. No one confronts the teacher.

As we read the wife's story we see how there is continuing psychological damage as the teenage victim is forced to be secretive, and eventually a wedge is forced between her and her parents and friends. These barriers or "wedges" are created between the molester and his wife and between the molester and his son. These "wedges" seem to be important in understanding the universe of damage that is created. Instead of openness and caring, the victim and the molester's family become isolated and secretive. At a difficult time, when the teenager is struggling with identity issues and emerging sexuality, she is forced to play games, to lie and keep secrets. She cannot talk over her problems with friends and family. Guilt and self-doubt are created. Instead of wrestling with a pimple-faced boy at a junior high prom, she is having intercourse with a teacher/father-figure boyfriend. The school environment, instead of being a safe haven for intellectual and social growth, becomes a mine or "mind" field of deception. Imagine the confusion and tension at a basketball game if you were a thirteen-year-old scorekeeper sitting next to the coach's wife, near your parents and classmates, right behind the thirty-year-old coach that you were secretly having sex with. Instead of the slow growth of the pubescent maturation process, you are embroiled in a sordid adult soap opera while you still have braces on your teeth. It might be difficult to handle these pressures and succeed academically. (Remember, often these chosen victims are having difficulties before the molester selects them.)

Also, we can begin to understand the dilemma of a wife who is a teacher. She has an allegiance to students, the community, and the school system. She is supposed to nurture and protect the students but also support and nurture her husband. Can she confront her husband? Can she go to the police or superintendent? Can she believe what she suspects, namely, that the man she loves, the father of her son, is lying to her and choosing to have sex with a thirteen-year-old student? Her doubts, her anger, her sense of isolation are a great burden. In this case, a suicide attempt is a momentary act of desperation. What is the effect on the teacher's son? The wife and son are abandoned or diminished by the teacher's interest in this other child. Can they be proud of their father, or when the abuse becomes public can they defend him? Can they express anger at him? Can they be friends with other children or do they too become a community pariah? Marital and sexual mores are confused or trashed. What happens to the relationship between the son and mother, and is she in a healthy enough state to support her son? Perhaps both parents are lost to the son and he is left isolated, confused, and angry.

As the wife discusses the trial we get some sense of the powerful tensions in the offender's family. He is depressed and minimizes his continuing problem. She is ambivalent as to whether she should support him or leave him. The awkwardness of all family members in a community aware of this case probably makes life difficult for all. Supporting an offender and his family is very risky. You might be seen as taking his side or being pro-rapist. The safest position for family, friends, or teaching colleagues is distance. Therefore, the wife and son may be isolated during these tense times. The wife appreciated the "space" that others gave her. She does not recall being attacked or rejected. It seems that her school colleagues acted with a good deal of dignity. From the wife's account we get validation of a major cornerstone of sex offender treatment.

The teacher explained his out-of-class student interactions as special attention that the student needed. We now call this "cognitive distortion." It is what the offender tells himself so that he can give himself permission to molest the student. He convinces himself that the student needs special attention. This assessment justifies, to himself, his actions. He is forming a special relationship with the victim for her own good. He feels that he is a self-sacrificing, dedicated teacher, not a sex offender abusing a young girl. This is a big part of the sex abuse cycle, which offenders learn about in treatment. Once identified, it helps them break the cycle if they want to.

As the wife ends her statement we are made aware of her continued anger at her husband and sadness for her son's loss, as well as the victim's psychological scars. She believes that better school procedures and better nationwide communications could reduce this problem. [Editor's Note: Because this section is taken verbatim from the wife, it has only been edited for punctuation and to change geographical locations.]

The wife speaks:

"I've been asked to speak to you about a certain kind of morals offense that we seem to be seeing more and more of lately, in and about our schools. This offense involves teachers taking sexual liberties with their students. I have been asked, in particular, to speak to you because I was personally involved in a case, and I hope in some way that the insight that I've gained through this experience will be able to benefit someone else.

"I think I'd like to start by giving you a little bit of a background into the relationship I had with my husband. Whether that has bearing on the case or not, I really don't know. But, just as a matter of background, we both married when we were very young. I was eighteen, my husband was nineteen. I was expecting my son at the time, so it was a marriage that was difficult in many ways. Financially, there were a lot of family pressures. He went to college and wanted to become a teacher. After he graduated from college, we decided to move away from the New Haven area. We liked Virginia a lot so that's where we decided to settle.

"His first teaching job in Virginia was at a junior high school. Junior high school students are anywhere from about twelve or thirteen to fifteen or sixteen years old, roughly speaking. I began to notice an unusual dedication to his job. He was a coach, so the coach's wives get used to spending a lot of time by themselves. They get used to long hours at practices, at games, and it's taken for granted that that is just part of your life when you are married to a teacher and a coach. I had other things in my life that were keeping me quite busy, such as my son. I was going back to school and I like to paint and do other things. So, really it wasn't an uncomfortable existence. It is just that he was gone a lot of the time. But, as I said, that was something that I came to expect. Well, besides being gone so much of the time we started getting phone calls at home. When I would answer the phone the other party would hang up. Then there would be games that he would say that he had to be at. Which, again, I'd expect. And I would find out later that there was no such game scheduled. There were weekends where he would be gone. He would go off for rides on his motorcycle, frequently, spending even less and less time at home. This was not an unusual procedure, though. Since the early days of our marriage, he was gone a lot. He was either at school or he was at work. We did take family vacations together, but there wasn't the usual father–son bonding, or there wasn't that real joy of being with each other. It seemed like he was always off doing something else. And there wasn't the time spent at home. So, this kind of continued that pattern where he was gone much of the time, and I just came to expect that he was giving as much to fatherhood as he could, and there just wasn't anything more to give.

"Anyway, the phone calls continued. Saying he was going to a game when there wasn't a game continued. I began to get more and more suspicious. He would mention kids in his class frequently. He would be out late at night. Finally, I think the first thing that really clued me in was when he would start taking his phone calls in the bedroom. He would not speak on the phone in front of me. He would go into the bedroom, close the door and pick up the phone. And he would be in there a long time. Well, jealousy, I guess was the main motivator, and there were a few times I picked up that phone and all I can say is, what I heard was a complete shock. It shouldn't have been. There was enough evidence there but I was just so—I just could not believe that someone could do this to me. I took it very personally. I took it as a personal failure. I took it as my fault and it was a major trial. The jealousy was the hardest emotion to deal with. The jealousy comes over you like a rage and there is no controlling that feeling at all. It's like a bit of madness. And, I'm just grateful that I lived through that period of my life, because there wasn't anything I wouldn't have done to keep that marriage together. When we did get married, I was young. I was an extremely devoted wife. There isn't anything he could do that I would say would be wrong. I just completely believed in him. So, when this happened, it was just utter disbelief that he could possibly, possibly be that kind of a person who would take advantage of a child. The girls I'm talking about in this case were thirteen and fourteen year olds.

"The biggest emotion I can think of, at that point, was shock and jealousy. I was extremely hurt. I felt unwanted, unloved. I didn't feel like I was good enough; that it was my fault that it had happened; that something I was doing was just not good enough. There was about a two-year depression that I went through at that time. My son was about four years old and a very demanding four year old. And I wasn't getting any support in that area at all, and to have this added on, on top, was just almost too much to bear. There were two years of deep depression. There was a suicide attempt on my part, where I took some sleeping pills. Luckily, it did not work. I think that suicide attempt was the turning point. I think after the—a few days after it was over and my stomach was still aching and it took a long, long time before my body recovered from that. I think, at that point, I decided to start taking care of myself first. It bothered me. It still bothers me, to this day, that even though I believed that he knew that I took some pills, it never occurred to him to call a hospital, to call a doctor. I remember him making me a cup of coffee and calling my brother-in-law on the phone and talking to my brother-in-law. And I remember his voice saying to me, 'You know you are really scaring him.' You know, and he used my husband's name. If I had been a little bit more conscious at the moment I would have said, 'Really, I'm scaring him. That's interesting.' But, anyway, we got through that point.

"There was a real effort to decide whether I wanted to go on with this marriage or not. I came to the conclusion I really loved my husband and that this might have just been a one-time event. It might have been due to being in a position of power with these kids where he had not experienced that before. And everyone is entitled to his or her mistakes. So, we decided to give it another try. We moved out of the area. Now, this first happened in Virginia. No charges were ever filed against him. He was told to resign or he would be fired. That was the choice he was given. To keep his record clean, he resigned. There was no paper trail at all. No evidence at all that any wrongdoing had been even attempted. So, we moved from Virginia. We moved back to New Haven. He worked as a substitute teacher in New Haven. To my knowledge, this did not occur again while we were back in New Haven. Of course, I can't be sure of this. But, looking back at those years. . . . We were back in New Haven for about two years, I don't recall any situation. We were also living near family then, too. Which I can imagine would make a difference in his susceptibility to this kind of problem—that with family around he might be a little bit more careful. Home life didn't change at all. He was still gone almost all the time. It was still—he was into his interests. I was the parent and I took care of the house, and I took care of all the domestic stuff and he was just into his own interests. And, that's basically how he has lived his life.

"After New Haven we moved to Idaho. He got a job teaching at a school district in the Salmon River Valley. There were several times when there would be students that I would worry about. And of course, I did worry about it. Because it happened once, it was always in the back of my mind. And I freely admit there was a lot of resentment there and a lot of hurt that I was never able to get rid of. Part of the reason I was never able to get rid of it, I believe, was because he never admitted it, even in Virginia. Listening on the phone, hearing the things he said, talking to those kids. He would get off of the phone and he would look at me like I was crazy for accusing him of ever doing anything, of hearing what I had heard. And he never admitted that he had done anything wrong, even though he lost his job over it. Even though we moved because of it. There was never that admission that he made a mistake, he did something wrong. And I think that's a big part of the problem, too.

"Anyway, we were back here in Idaho. There were occasions where I thought—I suspected that he might be starting a relationship again. I had no proof. Every time I would mention anything to him about seeing a kid, spending a lot of time away from home, he would get very upset with me. Say—ask me if I trusted him, ask me if he ever lied to me. And, of course, he had lied to me. But, that wasn't what he wanted to hear. He wanted to just erase what had happened in the past and wanted that blind faith back again, which I was finding it very difficult to give him. Every time I could I gave him that benefit of the doubt, though. I really didn't think anything happened the first few years we were there. I'm still not sure that anything happened the first few years. But, I do have very strong suspicions that there were several occasions where he did make advances towards students. The reason I believe that is because when he left the school district in the Salmon River Valley to take a job in Eastern Idaho, they were glad to get rid of him, frankly. These are things I heard later from several different teachers and administrators. No one ever said this to me at the time. This was all after the fact.

"He left the Salmon River Valley, worked at a school district in Eastern Idaho, worked in that school district for ten months and was asked to leave again. The reason he was asked to leave was because of alleged sexual innuendoes that he used during class and the way he treated the students. Now, this is the first time I had heard about a school commenting about his behavior. The way he explained it, it was just his East Coast mannerisms. It was unintentional. He certainly didn't mean anything by it, but that it was taken up in the wrong way. It was, after all, a small town he was working in. That's how it was explained to me.

"We moved back to the Salmon River Valley. He could not, as hard as he tried, get a job in the school district he left. This was my first feeling that something was going on before. Why wouldn't they take him back? He was supposed to be a, you know, a good coach and good teacher. Why wouldn't they want him back? He had a very difficult time trying to find a teaching position.

"After trying for several months, he got a job working at a fast food chain as a management trainee. He worked there for a little over a year. While working there, he was of course exposed again to teenage children and he became involved with one of the girls who worked at his store. This was more obvious to me. I remember him taking her out to movies while I was gone visiting my family back East. We didn't find out about this until later. But, he did take her to the movies. He even had the gall to bring my son along, I guess to provide a cover. Whatever.

I'm not sure. But, he was starting a relationship with her. I'm not sure how far that went. She was about sixteen years old.

"I, meanwhile, graduated and got a teaching job in another district in the Valley and started my teaching career. After I had taught for awhile I kept bringing my husband home job applications. He filled them out and sent them in and he was asked to interview for a job in the same district I worked in. He got the position. He started working at the middle-school level with hopes of moving up to the high school. He worked as a science teacher at the middle school.

"The phone calls started again; an uneasy feeling when he would be coaching. He was a basketball coach, and I remember going to the games and sitting next to the scorekeeper's box and next to the statisticians and there was just a very, very uncomfortable feeling. It's really hard to explain. It's like when you walk into a room and nobody wants to look you in the eye. They just want to look away from you. Up until that point, I was a very popular teacher. And I saw no reason why people were seemingly avoiding me. I just didn't make that connection. Phone calls started again. He was gone almost all the time. The difference, this time, was that he learned from his previous experiences and every time he suspected something was going to come up to diminish his credibility, he came up with a counteracting story. Like this child was having trouble with their schoolwork. He was going to meet them at the library, in a public place, so I wouldn't have to worry about it and nobody would think the wrong thing. And he would be helping her with her homework. Or, another case was where a child was having difficulty with her parents. A lot of emotional problems. He was on the phone almost nightly to the girl and the family trying to patch things up together. He was acting as a counselor. In fact, in almost all the cases where he did get sexually involved with his students, they were students that had some problem. Some problem that he could—it's a hard word to use but, I'm afraid it's the only fair one I can think of—he used their problems to—he exploited their problems for his own benefit. I believe to this day, he feels he was doing them a favor. But, I think we both know better that he was using these children because they were in a state where they needed someone. They wanted the comforting adult. They wanted someone to care. I'm sure it didn't enter those kids' minds that they were getting themselves involved in a physical relationship. I don't think it started like that in their minds, at all. I think they were lured.

"What I found out later was that there were several relationships with students at the middle-school level. The youngest was twelve-and-a-half. The oldest, I believe, was sixteen. She was a high school student. Again, these were troubled students. They turned to him for help and he used them physically. It still amazes me the gall in which he proceeded in these relationships. One of the student's fathers is an attorney. The mother is very involved in the school district. The other family thought my husband was a godsend because he was—it seemed to be—he was straightening out the family and helping them, and was this wonderful, caring, person. In fact, the mother was so impressed with him that she actually wrote a letter commending him to the school board and delivered it to the school board in person. This is the kind of effect he had on people. He is a very charismatic person. It is awfully hard to explain if you have never met him. But, you would never think that this person would do anything wrong. He just gives that image of always being the caring type, of always being the person to give more than 100 percent, always being the devoted coach, the devoted teacher, the devoted husband, devoted parent. And it has become quite evident that he was devoted at none of those things.

"Well, it turned out he did have affairs with several of his students. The statistician I sat next to at those basketball games was a student he was having an affair with for over two years, until she graduated high school and went on to the University of Nevada. It amazed me that I would be sitting next to her at games and how cool he was. This is how confident he was of being able to pull the wool over my eyes. That nobody was going to say anything. After all, who would say anything? Who would tell the wife? People don't. Fellow coaches and, I'm afraid, a lot of male teachers covered up for him, or, at least, they looked the other way. I don't believe they did it intentionally. I believe they were embarrassed. I believe they didn't know what to do. I also believe that they did not put the welfare of their students first. That they put the reputation of a colleague before the students. And I believe that was wrong. I believe the student has to come first. You give people a reasonable doubt. You talk to them. You ask them what is going on. But, if you feel that something improper is going on, that somehow that teacher is breaching that relationship, crossing over that line, I believe it is your duty to inform someone of your suspicions. You just can't turn the other way. And that's what I saw happen in his first school district. That's what I saw happen in the second school district he worked in where he also was asked to resign without any paper trail at all. It was only this very last district that he worked in that followed the correct procedures. They called in CPS [Child Protective Services]. They called the police department. That started the investigation that finally revealed his problem. But it wasn't until that third school district. And this is only the third one I know of where the problem existed.

"I remember taking students with us on different family outings. One in particular, a ski trip where I observed my husband acting in a very seductive manner with one of the students. I did talk to him about it. After the ski trip I refused to let this student call the home. I said I did not want phone calls coming home. Whenever a phone call would come from a female student I would instantly go back those ten years to the previous experience. And it would bring back such awful memories that I just told him I could not handle having students call at home. If he had to talk to students it would have to be at school. Still, there was that seductive behavior with the student and still, I turned away. I did not look. I did not want to believe that it could possibly ever happen again. After all, that was a long time ago and I had thought that after all these years we had built something, something that was worth hanging on to, was worth working with. I will admit to some problems in our marriage. There were problems with him being gone all the time. There were problems with him not being a caring parent. There were problems with me as far as resentments I was never able to get rid of. And I do admit to carrying those resentments around with me. They did affect us in many ways. They affected our sex life. They affected our relationship with our son. My son was one area that I felt that I was always strong with; that this was one area that he could not push me around. This was one area where I wanted to have my way with him. After all those years of marriage—this was about year fourteen—after all those years of marriage I had come to the point of not arguing with him when we had a difference of opinion. He was gone so much. It was really quite easy just to do things the way I wanted to do them. And that's exactly what happened. He was gone a lot so I took care of things. So I had my existence which, I don't know if I could use the term happy, because I don't believe I was happy. Something was missing from my life. I didn't have the closeness, I didn't have the trust, I didn't feel like it was an honest relationship with someone.

"While the second time everything blew up, the first time I had heard about it was the day he was called into the principal's office and shown the charges. Let me back track a little bit. The previous spring, one of the children he was dealing with went to see a private counselor. She had told the counselor that my husband had gotten physical with her and they would be kissing and necking, basically is what she told the counselor. The counselor informed the school and the student's parents. At that point, they all got together and—I didn't find this out until later—that my husband had gotten in touch with the student and intimidated her into retracting her story. This was really hard for me to imagine: the student and her parents, the counselor, and my husband in the same room. She apologized to him for lying. And she wasn't lying, she was telling the truth. I don't think he can ever appreciate what that child must have gone through. I don't think he ever really felt like he was hurting anyone, because none of the girls involved ever said no. He would intimidate them. He would seduce them. Because they were thirteen, because they were fourteen, they just didn't have the mental equipment to fight back. They didn't know what they wanted and here someone was offering them warmth and love, and they accepted it. It's hard to believe, looking back, what he could get them to do for him; what he could get the parents to do for him because they believed in him.

"Going back to the second time, now. I found out about it the day he was called into the principal's office. He came home. Well, he called me on the phone first, at school and said, 'Could you come home right away after school?', and I thought something had happened to our son. He said, 'No, no, no. It's just some school business that we need to talk about.' So I came home and he told me what the charges were against him. He denied the charges. He said that the child was fabricating the story, just as he had told me that the child the previous spring was fabricating the story. We didn't know what was going to happen. I wasn't sure what to feel or what to think. In the back of my mind I just remember thinking, not again. We're not going to go through this again. Several days later, the police became involved. They started their investigation. Within several weeks it became apparent that he was going to be formally charged and there would be a trial. At that point, he called up a lawyer through the state educational association. He made an appointment with the lawyer. That was the day, also, that he confessed to me that the charges were true and that he was involved with this student. I think that's when we separated. It was that day that he told me that the charges were true; that he had lied to me before. That's when I moved out of the bedroom and moved into one of the extra rooms by myself. I was still there. We still lived together for the rest of that school year. I couldn't see asking him to leave. He was totally devastated. I think having to tell the truth was part of the reason he was devastated. I remember going to the lawyer's office that day and sitting in the chair. He had just told me about that one student's charge, the charge he was going to be brought up on. In the lawyer's office, he told the lawyer about four students that he had been involved with since the time he taught in the district that I was teaching in; four students that I was hearing about for the first time in the lawyer's office. It was all I could do to keep from slipping out of the chair. I could not believe that he was being honest at this point because he feared—he feared that they would be putting him in jail. He wanted the lawyer to have all the information he could give him so he could best defend him. He did not tell the lawyer about the previous experiences in Virginia. He did not tell the lawyer about the person he was involved with at the fast food chain, but he did tell the lawyer about all the involvements he had just in that one school district, the same one I worked for.

"Time went on. He was asked to leave his classroom immediately. He was put on sick leave. The trial took forever. I was, of course, still teaching. I had to go into different schools and observe other teachers. One of the schools I had to go into was a school he had taught at. Looking back, I can't believe I had the guts to do it but I did, and I'm glad I did. But it was very, very hard at the time to go back into his school where the kids did know me and the other teachers did know me. The trial took an awful long time. I believe it was four or five months before he finally came to trial. At that point, they had plea-bargained. There were two students, now, ready to file charges. The second one would not unless he pleaded not guilty. In that case, that second student would have filed a case of statutory rape. That was what they used to plea-bargain. He pleaded guilty to a lesser charge, was given two years of probation and 100 hours of community service.

"I think the part that really made me cold, the part that was hardest for me to take, was reading the newspaper accounts of the trial, of the case against him. In particular, I remember one article in which the charges were listed incorrectly. It was a minor difference. He had gotten the charges lessened and the newspaper reported them as the stronger charge. I remember him reading the article and getting very upset at the newspaper. How dare they print the wrong thing. Something just went stone cold inside of me. I thought, how dare you. You were guilty of much worse than you are being charged with. You plea-bargained down to this. How could you possibly be that arrogant to be upset at the newspaper article that they were misquoting someone? Or that they had the charges listed incorrectly? How could you possibly be upset at that? Already, I could see that he was starting to cover things up, that he was starting to minimize. This is something he had done all along that I can see now is a pattern of his behavior. When something would happen, he would always minimize its effects. I wasn't really doing this to that child. I was only trying to do something else, trying to help. It wasn't important. He didn't hurt the children. That's what he wanted to believe: that he did not hurt them, that he only had their best interest at heart, and that really wasn't such a big deal. After all, in some places people get married at thirteen. What's the big deal?

"During the time of the charges and the trial and the sentencing, he was extremely depressed. He arranged to start seeing a psychologist before the charges were even filed. He felt that by seeing the psychologist initially that it would help his case. That he could say, 'See I'm already seeing someone. You know there is no reason to put me in jail. I'm dealing with this problem myself.' Of course he wasn't. It was just for show. He went to the psychologist for almost that entire school year until at the end of the school year when the psychologist initially said he couldn't help him if he was not willing to help himself. He was just going through the motions of going there. He was not really dealing with his problems. During this period of time, the psychologist did help a lot in helping him deal with his depression. He had terrible fits of depression. Crying. He talked about suicide frequently. He felt his whole life was coming apart. I'm sure he felt the distance between us, which started that very first day, and which grew with his confession, which grew with his reaction to the newspaper articles, which grew when I would just watch him. And I could see him in a whole different light, now. It was like seeing him from a distance and being able to tell how he operated a little bit better. Before, I was just too close to see. You wear blinders. And I just did not realize how he operated, how his mind worked, until I could separate myself emotionally from him.

"We stayed together, as far as in the same house, although we were separated, for the remainder of that year. He went out looking for another job because it was time for him to move out. At the end of the school year I went to see the psychologist several times to decide what I wanted to do with my life. I decided I did not want to be married to this person again. I felt very sure, as I feel sure right now that this is a pattern of behavior that will continue. This is not something that will just go away by itself. It is a problem, a compulsion that needs long-term treatment to cure. Not to cure, to control. I feel like he will always have that compulsion and given the chance, without facing up to his problem he is going to repeat his problem. I would not allow myself to become a part of that again. I would not allow myself to be emotionally involved with this person again, to put myself at such high a risk. I would not put my son through what he went through that year. He was the same age as the students my husband was involved with. It was very difficult for him because my husband was a coach. All the coaches knew each other. This was a case that was very well known within the school district. It was lesser known in public, although there were some occasions where I would go into a doctor's office and I would see people pointing and talking. The receptionist at my dentist's office would talk to me about it. Most people did not know me walking on the street, but everyone in the school knew what was going on. So, it was a very difficult, difficult time for us. I did not want to be married. I was very sure. I did not want to be married to this person any longer. If he could not face his problems, if he could not give it that much effort, I wasn't going to give our marriage any effort anymore, either.

"One thing I'd like to say about the school districts. They were very, very protective of me. I was a schoolteacher in the same district and I was protected. I was covered. I had like a blanket around me all the time. I had loving people around me who did everything they could to make life easier for me. School became a shelter. The way they decided to handle it was to let me go on with my normal life at school: to not discuss the problem, to let me just enjoy what I loved doing, teach, and that became my shelter. I think that was the best thing they could have done for me. That gave me a space where I could get strong again, and I'll always be grateful to them.

"Looking back, again, to these times I feel like my first experience with this problem was where I was weakest, where I was most vulnerable. After coming through that point, I felt like I've gotten a lot stronger. The second time I went through this problem I surprised myself. I surprised myself by the way I was able to carry on with my job, with taking care of my son, with facing people and being honest with people and with still being able to treat my ex-husband as a human being, being there when he was so depressed. I was truly amazed afterwards, looking back and seeing how strong I had become. I think it was because I was not as emotionally involved. I had done that distance. I had distanced myself from him, and I think that's what helped me cope with it.

"Afterthoughts. I do have some afterthoughts about his problem. Possibly, some of it might go further back than before we met, possibly into his teenage years. I believe he is a risk taker–type person. He wanted to risk his family. We were excellent cover for him. He had everything going for him. He had a job. He had a good job. He had a family that loved him. Everything seemed to be going well. Yet, all throughout the sixteen and a half years of our marriage, whenever things would start going well, something would happen to put that at risk. It was usually a car accident. Or it was usually a big expense he just had to have. Or, it was one of these cases that came up. It was almost like a marriage by trial. By one crisis after another crisis, after another crisis, and that seemed to be the way we held together. The rest of the family really did not know what was going on. They didn't know about all the difficulties. He was also a very, very, very private person. He did not want anyone else in the family to know what was going on. He, himself, did not tell his parents we were separated. He didn't tell them we were getting a divorce until I had actually filed for the divorce. His parents, I know, still—his mother at least, I know, still resents not being told what was going on sooner.

"It seemed that when everything was going well in our marriage, something would be risked. He needed to take that risk, to continue to take that risk. So being found out, caught, so to speak, and losing his family was very difficult for him. He could not stay in the area. This was another pattern that I've seen before. When he did get into trouble, he would want to move. He would want to get out of the area. He moved from New Haven to Virginia, Virginia back to New Haven, New

Haven to the Salmon River Valley, Salmon River Valley to
Eastern Idaho, then back to the Valley again. And since our
divorce he has moved at least two other times that I'm aware
of.

"To continue this story, I've been divorced a year, now. Shortly
after the divorce—I'd say eight months after the divorce—he
remarried. He remarried a woman with several teenagers, all
male. We did check on that. She seems to be the type of person
that I was years ago as far as being totally devoted to him. She
left her job, she left her home, and she traveled across several
states to be with him when he was just looking for a job, when
he had just found his first job, again. I guess that's what he
needs. He needs someone to be dependent on him. He needs
someone to be totally devoted to him. From things I have heard
since the divorce, I am confident that he has not changed. I am
confident that the pattern is still there. Whether he can control
it or not, that's anybody's guess. I say the odds are not in his
favor, not without getting the help that he needs. He has kind
of brushed it under the carpet. He has not dealt with his
problem. He has, again, set himself up in a situation where he
has a lot to lose. I think that the temptation to take that risk
again might be overwhelming.

"A few afterthoughts. For myself, I try very hard not to dwell
on the past. I went through a period of a lot of guilt. Being
another teacher was very difficult, was very difficult to handle
this. Because besides having your husband be unfaithful to
you, he was being unfaithful to you with a student, which
violated a professional ethic. So I was angry at a whole bunch
of different levels. I was angry for being used, I was angry that
he was unfair to me and that he had fooled around, I was angry
that he had misused his position of teacher. The power that
position holds is enormous, especially with the younger children and the middle-school children. He misused that power
to his own advantage, and I don't think I could have ever
forgiven him for that. That's where some of my guilt came in,
not being able to say anything, not being able to confront him.
But then, I think a little bit more about it and there were times
I did confront him. There were times I talked to him about it
and he would look at me straight in the face and lie. What could

you do? Unless I went chasing after him with a camera, unless I went following him, unless I got obsessive about it. Maybe I should have done that. But I try not to think about the things I should have done and I try to feel good about the things I was able to do.

"Legally, I've been collecting articles since this has happened to me about what local officials feel should be done about this problem. I don't see teacher fingerprinting as helping. I see the break in the chain of communications being between the administration and the teachers: that these cases are not being reported; that the administration of the school districts are allowing these teachers to resign and move on without any charges being filed, without any complaints being filed, and they are leaving one district, going into another district. The new district is totally unaware of the problems involved. In one of the articles, I believe, they said they knew what was going on as far as districts talking to each other, and they know what is happening, and that's just garbage. When he has moved from Virginia to New Haven to Idaho. No. We don't just pick up the phone and talk to each other. You can get buried.

"I would still worry that he will reapply for his teaching license and that in a few years, or maybe even next year, because he is entitled to reapply at this point, that he may get his teaching license back again, that possibly he could find a district somewhere and give some reason for not teaching for awhile and get back into a classroom. I still worry about that, and I try to keep tabs on him, to monitor what positions he is in, what job he is in, to make sure it's not at least directly involved with students.

"Fingerprinting will not work. Not alone. It has to start at the school-district level. These cases must be reported. They must be researched. There must be some proof as to whether the teacher is, in fact, guilty or the student possibly is making up the story, and I do believe that happens, too. Give that teacher the benefit of the doubt, but conduct an investigation. Keep that paper in that teacher's file, at least so another school district would be aware that something did come up. Now, with the first charge, with the first bit of paper in that teacher's file, that should not be enough to keep that person from teaching if the facts were not substantiated. It might just be the students seeking some kind of revenge against a teacher. But, as that teacher moves around, if more cases are found, the paperwork is added to the file, a pattern starts to emerge. I think that's when you find these teachers. We try so hard to protect their reputations. You know, we're going to be facing a teaching shortage. I don't believe a person would be kept out of teaching from one black Nate in their file. It's true that when something like this does come up, the first thing you think is the teacher is guilty. Being a parent, and being another teacher you can understand that possibly it could be the student that is getting their revenge in this way. I think it has to be the overall pattern that emerges from district to district that follows that teacher around that should be the main basis for looking at that teacher's behavior, possibly filing charges if the behavior happens again. At least, investigate. The hardest thing for me to deal with through this whole thing was knowing that he had this problem before, knowing there was no proof. He had this problem twice before with no proof. The district that I work for, the district that hired him had no way of knowing that he had this compulsion. They were really misled. They were really robbed. They were not getting the teacher they thought they were getting. So it is to the benefit of the school districts, for sure. It is for the benefit of the other teachers. It is for the benefit, most of all of those students to make sure that teacher's backgrounds are checked; that these instances are included in their paperwork and do follow them around from district to district. It's our students that we are trying to protect. This position of being a middle school and high school teacher is a very powerful position. A lot of the students are very, very attractive. They've grown up physically before they've grown up mentally. It would be easy for some people, if they have the compulsion already, to cross over that line and to take advantage of these students. Easy picking. Especially if the student has a problem. Many of them, today, do. Just being a teenager can be a problem. It's just too easy to abuse them.

"One of the things that was also mentioned in the article was that the fingerprinting was not necessary because you have intense personal contact with job applicant's references and past employers. That's not always true. For instance, one of the districts that he had a problem with is right next to another district he got a job with. Where is that personal contact? Why didn't someone from the first district say something to someone from the second district? I think without that paper trail people will turn their heads, they will say, 'Oh he's over that now. He won't do it again.' Or, if he did make a deal with the previous district, they would be able to find it out. That's not a risky case. In this particular case he took a coaching job away from our area and then came back again. You can't always tell. They didn't know that he made a deal with two previous districts. They hired him anyway. There is our lack of communication. There is our weakest link, and I think that is the area that I would focus on if I were trying to make the system work better. And I think the system has to work better. We are going to face a teacher shortage. I cringe at the thought of having him in a classroom again. I don't know what I would do if I ever found out that he was considering teaching again. And he is not alone. Most of these cases do not get reported. Most of these cases never come to trial. Most of these teachers move from one district to the next making these kinds of deals and going on with their behavior and the truth is, the truth as I believe it is, without intensive counseling, without wanting to change, without a long-term commitment to change your behavior, this is going to continue given the opportunity.

"I hope that I've been able to help in some small way. There are so many victims when something like this happens. There is, of course, that student victim who is uppermost in our minds, the person we are most concerned about. Then there is the person who is committing the offense. They are a victim too. Beyond that there is the family of the victim. I can't even imagine what I would have done had I been the mother of that little girl. I don't believe I would have been able to control my anger or my rage at someone taking advantage of my child in that way. This is a hurt that they are going to live with for the rest of their lives and certainly that little girl is going to live with for the rest of her life. Then there is the family of the sex offender himself. You can imagine the strain on a marriage. It did not break up my marriage. Not the case. His behavior broke up my marriage and his reluctance to change. This is something I'm always going to remember. It has been a growing experience for me. I would never want anyone to go through an experience like this again. For my son, it was very hard. He is pulling his life together, but it's going to take awhile and he will never have a relationship with his father, a warm, loving relationship. I am jealous sometimes when I see families where the father obviously enjoys being a father, enjoys their children and it's just a beautiful, beautiful thing to watch. I know my son is not going to have that. I honestly don't think he will ever be able to attain that father–son relationship. There are a lot of victims. The school district is a victim, too. Their reputation is injured. Teaching profession itself becomes a victim, and society in general becomes a victim when we trust our children to people who cannot be trusted.

"I hope that there will be a law that requires the paper trail I've described. I believe that would help. I know there are a lot of people interested in the problem now. I hope this has not just become a bit of a media event, and that it will have its share of time in the spotlight and then disappear. This isn't a problem that is going to go away. Schools are not easy places. Being a teenager is not an easy time of your life. We need to protect them. When I'm teaching my first graders about sexual abuse, I'll always have my experiences in the back of my mind, thinking that I want to make sure that these kids can stand up for themselves; that if something like this would happen to them at the middle school, that they would be able to say no; that they would be able to stand up for themselves. But even though I can teach them to say no, now, and I could teach them how to be strong now, those middle-school years are so difficult and they are so confused and they want so much for someone to love them. Unless we protect them I don't know if they will have the strength to protect themselves. It is a very vulnerable part of their life, and I think that is what we need to focus on is protecting those kids."

AT press time, an important Supreme Court decision was handed down, regarding a case involving a consensual sexual relationship between a student and teacher. A discussion of it has been added here because of its timeliness and because of the possible ramifications that may result because of the decision.

On June 22, 1998, the United States Supreme Court issued a 5–4 decision in *Gebser v. Lago Vista Independent School Dist.*,[25] a case involving a consensual sexual relationship between 15-year-old Alida Star Gebser and her 52-year-old teacher Frank Waldrop. Their sexual relationship went on for 6 months and involved repetitive sexual contacts, including some during school hours but away from school grounds. The affair ended when a police officer found the two nude and actively engaged in sexual intercourse. Alida Star, who later joined her mother in the lawsuit against the school district and officials, admitted that she had told no one, including her mother, about the relationship. Three months earlier, two other female students had reported to their parents Mr. Waldrop's in-class sexual comments, and the parents complained to the school principal. Thereafter, the principal arranged a meeting between Mr. Waldrop and the parents, at

---

[25] 118 S.Ct. 1989, ____ L.Ed. 2d. _____ , 125 Ed. Law Rpt. 1055, 66 U.S.L.W. 4501, LEXIS 4173 (1998).

which Mr. Waldrop, while denying he had been improper, apologized for the comments. The principal did not report the complaints to the superintendent, who was also the school district's Title IX compliance officer.

Based upon these facts, the trial court concluded that there was insufficient evidence that the school district or its officials had *actual* knowledge of a Title IX violation.[26] The trial court also ruled that "constructive notice" (knew or should have known) should not be applied in a Title IX claim and similarly chose not to apply vicarious liability to the employer for acts of its agent, Frank Waldrop (the respondeat superior concept). Thereafter, the United States Court of Appeals for the Fifth Circuit upheld the trial court,[27] and the matter was appealed to the United States Supreme Court.

The *Gebser* decision has generated considerable comment and at least some misunderstanding. This text (see especially Chapter 7) endorses application of the "knew or should have known" standard[28] which the *Gebser* Court first acknowledges and then specifically rejects as the applicable standard. Complaints about this teacher from others 3 months before the sexual relationship was exposed is the sort of knowledge we (the authors) espouse as sufficient to create a "reasonable suspicion" requiring that the administration look further. Also, the *Gebser* opinion focuses on *actual individual knowledge* rather than collective corporate knowledge of the school district.[29] *Gebser* emphasizes that the principal did not tell the superintendent, who was the Title IX compliance officer; thus, the person in a position to abate the risk to the educational environment did not know what the principal knew. In particu-

---

[26]Title IX, Rev. Statute, 20 U.C.S. 168(a) prohibits "discrimination under any education program or activity receiving Federal financial assistance" and applies to all public school systems.

[27]*Doe v. Lago Vista Independent School Dist.*, 106 F. 3d 1223 (1997).

[28]United States Department of Education, Office of Civil Rights, "Policy Guidance," 62 *Fed. Reg.* 12034, 12039 (1997).

[29]Ibid. When a "responsible person" in the employ of the school district knows or should know that sexual abuse is occurring, the Office of Civil Rights (OCR) considers the school district to know what the person knew or should have known.

lar, distinguishing between the principal and the superintendent, the Court said:

> We hold that a damages remedy will not lie under Title IX unless
> an official who at a minimum has authority to address the
> alleged discrimination and to institute corrective measures on
> the recipient's behalf has actual knowledge of discrimination in
> the recipient's programs and fails adequately to respond.
>
> We think, moreover, that the response must amount to deliber-
> ate indifference to discrimination. The administrative enforce-
> ment scheme presupposes that an official who is advised of a
> Title IX violation refuses to take action to bring the recipient
> into compliance. (1999 S.Ct.)

A superficial reading of *Gebser* appears to endorse the "head
in sand" mentality, which historically resulted in few staff
dismissals for sexual abuse of students. In particular, why not
replicate *Gebser* by designating the superintendent as Title IX
compliance officer and then finding innovative reasons not to
tell the superintendent when sexual abuse or harassment
complaints are made? The answer is simple: subordinate administrators who participate in that solution are being deliberately indifferent; they are exposing themselves to *personal
liability*, and therefore, ignoring and not reporting complaints
won't work.

Administrators who want a stable, secure, and successful
career in public school administration must apply the "knew
or should have known" (constructive notice) standard. Subor-
dinates *must* be held to this standard. There is no salvation in
avoiding reality. Students who are sexually abused by teachers
eventually become plaintiffs in lawsuits against teachers, administrators, and school districts. Because of the decision in
Gebser, lawyers raising Title IX damage claims will now claim
supervising administrators had *actual knowledge*.[30] In order to
avoid the consequences of *Gebser*, trial courts will allow *actual
knowledge* claims to go to the jury. Win or lose, the administrator who is the target of claims of this sort will ultimately

---

[30]In *Gebser*, the Court cited *Franklin v. Gwinnett County Public Schools*, 503
U.S. 60 (1992), wherein the Court had ruled that Title IX could be enforced
with a money damage claim. Such claims are still viable.

lose. Alternatively, claims for prospective equitable (injunctive) Title IX relief will be based upon the "knew or should have known" standard, or claims will be based in state law, allowing the constructive notice standard in negligence claims. *Gebser* applies to money damage claims, not claims for prospective injunctive relief. *Gebser* does not preclude a state-law-based constructive notice or respondeat superior claim. Finally, OCR continues to apply the constructive notice standard in Title IX enforcement actions.

Abel, G. G., Osborne, C. A., and Twigg, D. A. (1993). Sexual assault through the lifespan. In H. E. Barbaree, W. L. Marshall and S. M. Hudson (Eds.), *The Juvenile Sex Offender* (pp. 104–116). New York: The Guilford Press.

Anderson, D. (1979). Touching; when is it caring and nurturing or when is it exploitative and damaging. *Child Abuse and Neglect, 3,* 793–794.

Baker, A. W. and Duncan, S. P. (1985). Child sexual abuse: A study of prevalence in Great Britain. *Child Abuse and Neglect, 9,* 457–467.

Bandura, A. (1977). *Social Learning Theory.* Englewood Cliffs, N.J.: Prentice-Hall. Bartholomew, K. (1990). Avoidance of intimacy: An attachment perspective. *Journal of Social and Personal Relationships, 7,* 147–148.

Bartholomew, K. and Horowitz, L. M. (1991). Attachment styles among adults: A test of a four category model. *Journal of Personality and Social Psychology,* 61, 226–244.

Berrick, J. D. (1988). Parental involvement in child abuse prevention training: what do they learn? *Child Abuse and Neglect,* 12, 543–553.

Becker, J. V., Alpert, J. L., Bigfoot, D. S., and Walker, F. L. (1995). Empirical research on child abuse treatment. *Journal of Clinical Child Psychology,* 24, 23–46.

Bowlby, J. (1969). *Attachment and Loss. Volume I: Attachment.* New York: Basic Books.

Bork, R. (1996). *Slouching towards Gomorrah.* New York: Harper-Collins.

Bukowski, W. M., Sippola, L., and Brender, W. (1993). Where does sexuality come from?: Normative sexuality from a developmental perspective. In H. E. Barbaree, W. L. Marshall, and S. M. Hudson (Eds.), *The Juvenile Sex Offender* (pp. 84–100). New York: The Guilford Press.

Coleman, L. (1986) False allegations of child sexual abuse: Have the experts been caught with their pants down? *Forum,* January–February.

Coleman, L. (1994). The manufacture of sexual abuse memories: Psychiatry's latest fad. In L. Krivascica and J. Money (Eds.), *Handbook of Forensic Sexology.* Amherst, N.Y.: Prometheus Books.

Crewden, J. (1988). *By Silence Betrayed*. Boston: Little, Brown, and Company.

Dolmage, W.D. (1995). Accusations of teacher sexual abuse of students in Ontario schools: Some preliminary findings. *The Alberta Journal of Educational Research*, XLI, 2, 127–144.

Elkind, D. (1981). *The Hurried Child*. Reading, MA: Addison-Wesley.

Feeny, J. A. and Noller, P. (1990). Attachment styles as a predictor of adult, romantic relationships. *Journal of Personality and Social Psychology*, 58, 281–289.

Finklehor, D. (1984). *Child Sexual Abuse*. New York: The Free Press.

Finklehor, D. (1986). *A Sourcebook on Child Sexual Abuse*. Beverly Hills, CA: Sage Publications.

Fraser, B. G. (1981). *Sexual Abuse: The Legislation and Law in the United States*, cited in Mrazek, P. B. and Kempe, C. H. (Eds.) *Sexually Abused Children and Their Families*. New York: Pergamon.

Gilbert, N. (1988). Teaching children to prevent sexual abuse. *The Public Interest*, 93, 3–15.

Groth, N. (1979). *Men Who Rape*. New York: Plenum.

Haugaard, J. J. and Reppucci, N. D. (1988). *A Comprehensive Guide to Current Knowledge and Intervention Strategies*. San Francisco: Jossey-Bass.

Hazen, C. and Shaver, P. (1994). Attachment as an organizational framework for research on close relationships. *Psychological Inquiry*, 5, 1–22.

Hechler, D. (1988). *The Battle and the Backlash*. Lexington, MA.: D.C. Heath and Co.

Hindman, J. (1987). *Step by Step*. Ontario, Oregon: Alex Andria Associates.

Hyman, I. E. (1994). Conversational remembering: Story recall with a peer versus for an experimenter. *Applied Cognitive Psychology*, 8, 49–66.

Kempe, C. H. and Helfer, R. E. (1980). *The Battered Child*. Chicago: University of Chicago Press.

Kempe, R. S. and Kempe C. H. (1984). *The Common Secret: Sexual Abuse of Children and Adolescents*. New York: W. H. Freeman.

Kleemeier, C., Webb, C., Hazzard, A., and Pohl, J. (1988). *Child Abuse and Neglect*, 12, 555–561.

Lynch, M. A. (1985). Child abuse before Kempe: An historical literature review. *Child Abuse and Neglect*, 9, 7–15.

Loftus, E. F. (1992). When a lie becomes memory's truth: Memory distortion after exposure to misinformation. *Current Directions in Psychological Science*, 1, 121–123.

Loftus, E. F. (1993). The reality of repressed memories. *American Psychologist*, 48, 518–537.

MacFarlane, K. and Waterman, J. (1986). *The Sexual Abuse of Young Children: Evaluation and Treatment*. New York: The Guilford Press.

Marshall, W. L. and Eccles, A. (1993). Pavlovian conditioning processes in adolescent sex offenders. In Barbaree, H. D., Marshall, W. L., and

Hudson, S. M. (Eds.). *The Juvenile Sex Offender*. New York: The Guilford Press.

Marshall, W. L. Hudson, S. M., and Hodkinson, S. (1993). The importance of attachment bonds in the development of juvenile sex offending. In Barbaree, H. E., Marshall, W. L., and Hudson, S. M. (Eds.). *The Juvenile Sex Offender*. New York: The Guilford Press.

Matsakis, A. (1992). *I Can't Get Over It*. Okland, CA: New Harbinger.

McIntyre, T. C. (1987). Teacher awareness of child abuse and neglect. *Child Abuse and Neglect*, 11, 133–135.

Porch, T. L. and Petretic-Jackson, P. A. (1986, August). Child sexual assault prevention: Evaluating parent education workshops. Paper presented at the convention of the American Psychological Association. Washington, D.C.

Radbill, S. X. (1980). Children in a world of violence: A history of child abuse. In Kempe, C. H. and Helfer, R. E. (Eds.). *The Battered Child*. Chicago: The University of Chicago Press.

Rubin, S. (1988). *Sex Education: Teachers Who Sexually Abuse Students*. Paper presented at the 24th Annual International Congress of Psychology, Sydney, Australia.

Russell, D. E. H. (1983). Incidence and prevalence of intrafamilial and extrafamilial sexual abuse of female children. *Child Abuse and Neglect*, 7, 133–146.

Russell, D. E. H. (1986). *The Secret Trauma: Incest in the Lives of Girls and Women*. New York: Basic Books.

Sarafina, E. (1979). Estimates of sexual offenses against children. *Child Welfare*, 38, 127–133.

Scheter, M. D. and Roberge, L. (1976). Sexual exploitation. In Kempe, C. H. and Helfer, R. E. (Eds.). *Child Abuse and Neglect*. Cambridge, MA: Ballinger.

Sgroi, S. M. (Ed.) (1982). *Handbook of Clinical Intervention in Child Sexual Abuse*. Lexington, MA: Lexington Books.

Shakeshaft, C. and Cohan, A. (1995). Sexual abuse of students by school personnel. *Phi Delta Kappan*, March, 513–520.

Ward, T., Hudson, S. M., Marshall, W. L., and Siegert, R. (1995). Attachment style and intimacy deficits in sexual offenders: A theoretical framework. *Sexual Abuse: A Journal of Research and Treatment*, 7, 4, 317–333.

West, D. J. (1987). *Sexual Crimes and Confrontations*. Cambridge: University Press.

Winks, P. L. (1982). Legal implications of sexual contact between teacher and student. *Journal of Law and Education*, 11, 4, 437–477.

Wurtele, S. K. and Miller-Perrin, C. L. (1992). *Preventing Child Sexual Abuse*. Lincoln, Nebraska. University of Nebraska Press.